PRENTICE-HALL CONTEMPORARY
PERSPECTIVES IN PHILOSOPHY SERIES

Joel Feinberg and Wesley C. Salmon, *editors*

Alan Ross Anderson	MINDS AND MACHINES
V. C. Chappell	ORDINARY LANGUAGE
Nelson Pike	GOD AND EVIL
George Pitcher	TRUTH
Vincent Tomas	CREATIVITY IN THE ARTS

GOD AND EVIL

Readings on the Theological Problem of Evil

Edited by

NELSON PIKE

Cornell University

CONTEMPORARY PERSPECTIVES

IN PHILOSOPHY SERIES

PRENTICE-HALL, INC. Englewood Cliffs, New Jersey

PRENTICE-HALL INTERNATIONAL, INC., *London*
PRENTICE-HALL OF AUSTRALIA, PTY., LTD., *Sydney*
PRENTICE-HALL OF CANADA, LTD., *Toronto*
PRENTICE-HALL OF INDIA (PRIVATE) LTD., *New Delhi*
PRENTICE-HALL OF JAPAN, INC., *Tokyo*

© 1964
by PRENTICE-HALL, INC.
Englewood Cliffs, N.J.

Current printing (last digit):
19 18 17 16

Library of Congress Catalog Card Number:
64-11869

Printed in the United States of America
C-35766

CONTEMPORARY PERSPECTIVES

IN PHILOSOPHY

This series is designed to provide a wide group of readers with collections of essays by contemporary philosophers on problems presently under active discussion in philosophical circles. The articles have been carefully selected for their lucidity and intelligibility, revealing the vitality of current philosophy to an audience which would not normally have recourse to professional journals. Each volume consists of articles devoted to a single topic, thereby creating an unusual degree of internal coherence and dialectical unity. In many cases the articles are addressed to one another as replies or rebuttals, or are otherwise built upon earlier essays to carry the discussion forward to new levels of clarity. The editor of each volume contributes an introduction which furnishes the reader with the orientation and general framework for a full understanding of the issues. Although each volume is deliberately restricted in scope, the series as a whole ranges over the entire breadth of philosophy, from aesthetics and philosophy of religion to semantics and philosophy of science.

The series is dedicated to the view that contemporary philosophical perspectives—even on ancient problems—are distinctive, exciting, and fully intelligible to students and other nonprofessionals. The volumes are designed for use as supplementary materials or as components in larger "homemade" anthologies, in both introductory and advanced courses, and for use as basic source materials for student research projects. They enable the teacher to expose students to current philosophy without the usual struggle over library copies of journals. In addition, these anthologies will be useful to scholars in fields bordering on philosophy—for example, law, linguistics, literature, mathematics, physics, psychology, and theology—who wish to find in convenient capsule form the best of recent philosophical thinking on subjects of interest to them. For readers in general, the series provides an opportunity to sample the actual substance and methods of contemporary philosophy.

JOEL FEINBERG
Princeton University

WESLEY C. SALMON
Indiana University

CONTENTS

GOD AND EVIL

Readings on the Theological Problem of Evil

INTRODUCTION

Boethius asked: "If there be a God, from whence proceed so many evils?" [1] Boethius might have framed his question in greater detail as follows: If God is omnipotent, then He could prevent evil if He wanted to. And if God is perfectly good, then He would want to prevent evil if He could. Thus, if God exists and is both omnipotent and perfectly good, then there exists a being who *could* prevent evil if he *wanted to,* and who would *want to* prevent evil if he *could.* And if this last is true, how can there be so many evils in the world? This, in broad outline, is the traditional theological problem of evil. And it is to the many issues connected with this problem that the seven essays contained in this book are addressed.

---

[1] *Consultations of Philosophy,* Book I, Sec. IV.

1

The collection begins with a short chapter from Feodor Dostoevski's *The Brothers Karamazov.* In this selection Dostoevski sketches the problem in vivid—indeed pungent—strokes. The problem of evil is not a theological "puzzle." It is a problem which must touch the soul of every sensitive religious person. Dostoevski does not let us forget this fact.

The second selection is the many-faceted discussion of evil presented in Parts X and XI of David Hume's *Dialogues Concerning Natural Religion.* The center of this discussion is usually taken to be Part X. Here, Hume (in the person of Philo) argues that "God exists" and "evil exists" are logically incompatible propositions. One might put this point as follows: When Boethius asked: "If there be a God, from whence proceed so many evils," he was asking a question having the same logical status as: "If Jones is a bachelor, how does it happen that he has a wife?" The question, in other words, is not a genuine question. It *could not* have an answer. It is not just that evil in the world is hard to understand if one assumes the existence of the Judeo-Christian God. Hume's point is that evil in the world is *logically* incompatible with traditional theism. God and evil *could* not exist together in the same universe.

No sooner does Philo develop the idea that "God exists" and "evil exists" are logically incompatible propositions than he agrees to "retire" from this position and unexpectedly grants the claim that God could have created a universe containing evil. This move in Hume's discussion ought not to be misunderstood. I think Hume is convinced that "God exists" and "evil exists" *are* logically incompatible statements. But he also thinks that the existence of evil in the world would present a major problem for some theologians (i.e., the sort of theologian represented by Cleanthes in the *Dialogues*) even if it were agreed that there is no logical conflict between these two statements. In a theology in which the existence of God is presented as an *hypothesis* capable of having *evidence,* evil in the world constitutes strong evidence *against* the theistic hypothesis. Even if "God exists" and "evil exists" are logically compatible propositions, the fact that the latter is true provides good reason (though no longer conclusive reason) for thinking that the former is false. This is the thesis developed in Part XI of the *Dialogues.*

Hume's attack on traditional theism thus exhibits a double-layered structure. The first (and principal) claim is that "God exists" and "evil exists" are logically incompatible statements; thus, since evil exists, we can be sure that God does not exist. And the second (more guarded) claim is that even if "God exists" and "evil exists" are logically compatible statements, since evil exists, we have strong (though not conclusive) reason for thinking that God does not exist.

In the third selection, John Stuart Mill broadens the general antitheistic attack marked out by Hume. In both versions of his attack Hume took issue with the theologian who claims that there exists an all-powerful and perfectly good God—and who uses the term "good" in his theology in its ordinary, everyday sense. But what about the theologian (and there have been many) who affirms that God is perfectly good and who adds that the term "good" as applied to God does not have the meaning it has when applied to things other than God? God is infinitely good. Infinite goodness is beyond our comprehension. The finite mind can not grasp the goodness of God. The very word used to designate this attribute has a different *meaning* in theology than it has in other kinds of discourse. How, then, can Hume argue that if God is good, He would prevent evil if He could? This might hold (as an analytic truth) if "good" were used in its ordinary sense. But when speaking of God, "good" is not used in its ordinary sense. Mill exposes the theologically unfortunate consequences involved in this way of avoiding the problem of evil.

Two essays by J. L. Mackie and H. J. McCloskey develop the first of Hume's two positions down yet another track. Each begins with the claim that "God exists" and "evil exists" are logically incompatible propositions; and each goes on to examine a number of the attempts which have been made by theologians to explain why a perfectly good God permits evil to occur. Theologians, for the most part, have assumed that Boethius' opening question is a *bona fide* question. They have attempted to provide answers to it. Such attempts are called "theodicies." For example, Leibniz held that the world God has created is the best of all possible worlds. Though it might be hard for us to understand, each instance of evil contributes to the perfection of the world as a whole. Thus, to Boethius' question "If there be a God, from whence proceed so many evils?" Leibniz answered as follows: God permits evil to exist because were He to prevent it, as indeed He could if He wanted to, the world would not be as good as it could be. Of course, if Hume was right in thinking that "God exists" and "evil exists" are logically incompatible statements, Boethius' question *could* not have an answer. And from this it would follow that any proposed answer to it (such as the one given by Leibniz) must be conceptually deficient. If we simply assumed that Hume was right, we would not have to study the details of this or any other particular theodicy. We could know in advance that any such theory is logically defective. But the question remains whether Hume *was* right. And an important part of the argument for the position he advanced must consist of showing that the specific theodicies proposed by theologians are, in fact, defective. This is the task undertaken by Mackie and McCloskey. Between them they examine and reject most of the major theodicies used in the Western theological tradition.

The remaining two selections in the book are included as efforts to clarify the problem of evil via a protest of the general position worked out in the four essays just described. My own contribution contains a rather extensive examination of Hume's discussion of evil. I contend that Hume's central claim (viz., that the propositions "God exists" and "evil exists" are logically incompatible) has not been effectively argued, nor is it clear that it *can* be effectively argued. It is not at all obvious that God and evil could not exist together in the same universe. I then go on to suggest that if "God exists" and "evil exists" are logically *compatible* propositions, the problem of evil, as it arises in most historically important theologies, is not the critical theoretical issue it is often thought to be. An essay by Ninian Smart completes the collection. Smart undertakes an analysis of a favorite anti-theistic contention, namely, that God might have created men wholly good (i.e., incapable of immoral action), and that the world would have been better had He done so. Smart argues that it is quite unclear whether a world devoid of men capable of immoral action would be better than a world containing men who can (and do) perform morally offensive actions. Of course, Smart and I only sample the many objections which might be raised against the position developed in the earlier selections. But I think we do our bit toward a clarification of the issues. And perhaps we say enough to (at least) suggest that those who have advanced the celebrated "argument from evil" against the existence of God may not have had the last word on the topic.

REBELLION

FEODOR DOSTOEVSKI

"I must make you one confession," Ivan began. "I could never under-stand how one can love one's neighbors. It's just one's neighbors, to my mind, that one can't love, though one might love those at a distance. I once read somewhere of John the Merciful, a saint, that when a hungry, frozen beggar came to him, he took him into his bed, held him in his arms, and began breathing into his mouth, which was putrid and loathsome from some awful disease. I am convinced that he did that from 'self-laceration,' from the self-laceration of falsity, for the sake of the charity imposed by duty, as a penance laid on him. For any one to love a man, he must be hidden, for as soon as he shows his face, love is gone."

"Father Zossima has talked of that more than once," observed Alyosha,

From The Brothers Karamazov, *C. Garnett, trans., Book V, Chap. 4 (New York: Modern Library, Inc., 1950). Reprinted by permission of Random House, Inc.*

"he, too, said that the face of a man often hinders many people not practiced in love, from loving him. But yet there's a great deal of love in mankind, and almost Christ-like love. I know that myself, Ivan."

"Well, I know nothing of it so far, and can't understand it, and the innumerable mass of mankind are with me there. The question is, whether that's due to men's bad qualities or whether it's inherent in their nature. To my thinking, Christ-like love for men is a miracle impossible on earth. He was God. But we are not gods. Suppose I, for instance, suffer intensely. Another can never know how much I suffer, because he is another and not I. And what's more, a man is rarely ready to admit another's suffering (as though it were a distinction). Why won't he admit it, do you think? Because I smell unpleasant, because I have a stupid face, because I once trod on his foot. Besides there is suffering and suffering; degrading, humiliating suffering such as humbles me—hunger, for instance—my benefactor will perhaps allow me; but when you come to higher suffering—for an idea, for instance—he will very rarely admit that, perhaps because my face strikes him as not at all what he fancies a man should have who suffers for an idea. And so he deprives me instantly of his favor, and not at all from badness of heart. Beggars, especially genteel beggars, ought never to show themselves, but to ask for charity through the newspapers. One can love one's neighbors in the abstract, or even at a distance, but at close quarters it's almost impossible. If it were as on the stage, in the ballet, where if beggars come in they wear silken rags and tattered lace and beg for alms dancing gracefully, then one might like looking at them. But even then we should not love them. But enough of that. I simply wanted to show you my point of view. I meant to speak of the suffering of mankind generally, but we had better confine ourselves to the sufferings of the children. That reduces the scope of my argument to the tenth of what it would be. Still we'd better keep to the children, though it does weaken my case. But, in the first place, children can be loved even at close quarters, even when they are dirty, even when they are ugly (I fancy, though, children never are ugly). The second reason why I won't speak of grown-up people is that, besides being disgusting and unworthy of love, they have a compensation—they've eaten the apple and know good and evil, and they have become 'like god.' They go on eating it still. But the children haven't eaten anything, and are so far innocent. Are you fond of chil-

dren, Alyosha? I know you are, and you will understand why I prefer
to speak of them. If they, too, suffer horribly on earth, they must suffer
for their fathers' sins, they must be punished for their fathers, who have
eaten the apple; but that reasoning is of the other world and is incomprehensible for the heart of man here on earth. The innocent must not
suffer for another's sins, and especially such innocents! You may be
surprised at me, Alyosha, but I am awfully fond of children, too. And
observe, cruel people, the violent, the rapacious, the Karamazovs are
sometimes very fond of children. Children while they are quite little—
up to seven, for instance—are so remote from grown-up people; they are
different creatures, as it were, of a different species. I knew a criminal
in prison who had, in the course of his career as a burglar, murdered
whole families, including several children. But when he was in prison,
he had a strange affection for them. He spent all his time at his window,
watching the children playing in the prison yard. He trained one little
boy to come up to his window and made great friends with him . . .
You don't know why I am telling you all this, Alyosha? My head aches
and I am sad."

"You speak with a strange air," observed Alyosha uneasily, "as though
you were not quite yourself."

"By the way, a Bulgarian I met lately in Moscow," Ivan went on,
seeming not to hear his brother's words, "told me about the crimes committed by Turks and Circassians in all parts of Bulgaria through fear
of a general rising of the Slavs. They burn villages, murder, outrage
women and children, they nail their prisoners by the ears to the fences,
leave them so till morning, and in the morning they hang them—all
sorts of things you can't imagine. People talk sometimes of bestial cruelty, but that's a great injustice and insult to the beasts; a beast can
never be so cruel as a man, so artistically cruel. The tiger only tears and
gnaws, that's all he can do. He would never think of nailing people by
the ears, even if he were able to do it. These Turks took a pleasure in
torturing children, too; cutting the unborn child from the mother's
womb, and tossing babies up in the air and catching them on the points
of their bayonets before their mother's eyes. Doing it before the mother's
eyes was what gave zest to the amusement. Here is another scene that
I thought very interesting. Imagine a trembling mother with her baby
in her arms, a circle of invading Turks around her. They've planned a

diversion; they pet the baby, laugh to make it laugh. They succeed, the baby laughs. At that moment a Turk points a pistol four inches from the baby's face. The baby laughs with glee, holds out its little hands to the pistol, and he pulls the trigger in the baby's face and blows out its brains. Artistic, wasn't it? By the way, Turks are particularly fond of sweet things, they say."

"Brother, what are you driving at?" asked Alyosha.

"I think if the devil doesn't exist, but man has created him, he has created him in his own image and likeness."

"Just as he did God, then?" observed Alyosha.

" 'It's wonderful how you can turn words,' as Polonius says in *Hamlet*," laughed Ivan. "You turn my words against me. Well, I am glad. Yours must be a fine God, if man created Him in His image and likeness. You asked just now what I was driving at. You see, I am fond of collecting certain facts, and, would you believe, I even copy anecdotes of a certain sort from newspapers and books, and I've already got a fine collection. The Turks, of course, have gone into it, but they are foreigners. I have specimens from home that are even better than the Turks. You know we prefer beating—rods and scourges—that's our national institution. Nailing ears is unthinkable for us, for we are, after all, Europeans. But the rod and scourge we have always with us and they cannot be taken from us. Abroad now they scarcely do any beating. Manners are more humane, or laws have been passed, so that they don't dare to flog men now. But they make up for it in another way just as national as ours. And so national that it would be practically impossible among us, though I believe we are being inoculated with it, since the religious movement began in our aristocracy. I have a charming pamphlet, translated from the French, describing how, quite recently, five years ago, a murderer, Richard, was executed—a young man, I believe, of three and twenty, who repented and was converted to the Christian faith at the very scaffold. This Richard was an illegitimate child who was given as a child of six by his parents to some shepherds on the Swiss mountains. They brought him up to work for them. He grew up like a little wild beast among them. The shepherds taught him nothing, and scarcely fed or clothed him, but sent him out at seven to herd the flock in cold and wet, and no one hesitated or scrupled to treat him so. Quite the contrary, they thought they had every right, for Richard had been

given to them as a chattel, and they did not even see the necessity of
feeding him. Richard himself describes how in those years, like the
Prodigal Son in the Gospel, he longed to eat of the mash given to the
pigs, which were fattened for sale. But they wouldn't even give him
that, and beat him when he stole from the pigs. And that was how he
spent all his childhood and his youth, till he grew up and was strong
enough to go away and be a thief. The savage began to earn his living
as a day laborer in Geneva. He drank what he earned, he lived like a
brute, and finished by killing and robbing an old man. He was caught,
tried, and condemned to death. They are no sentimentalists there. And
in prison he was immediately surrounded by pastors, members of Christian brotherhoods, philanthropic ladies, and the like. They taught him to
read and write in prison, and expounded the Gospel to him. They ex-
horted him, worked upon him, drummed at him incessantly, till at last
he solemnly confessed his crime. He was converted. He wrote to the
court himself that he was a monster, but that in the end God had vouch-
safed him light and shown grace. All Geneva was in excitement about
him—all philanthropic and religious Geneva. All the aristocratic and
well-bred society of the town rushed to the prison, kissed Richard and embraced him: 'You are our brother, you have found grace.' And Richard
does nothing but weep with emotion, "Yes, I've found grace! All my
youth and childhood I was glad to have pigs' food, but now even I have
found grace. I am dying in the Lord.' 'Yes, Richard, die in the Lord;
you have shed blood and must die. Though it's not your fault that you
knew not the Lord, when you coveted the pigs' food and were beaten for
stealing it (which was very wrong of you, for stealing is forbidden); but
you've shed blood and you must die.' And on the last day, Richard, perfectly limp, did nothing but cry and repeat every minute: 'This is my
happiest day. I am going to the Lord.' 'Yes,' cry the pastors and the
judges and philanthropic ladies. 'This is the happiest day of your life,
for you are going to the Lord!' They all work or drive to the scaffold in
procession behind the prison van. At the scaffold they call to Richard:
'Die, brother, die in the Lord, for even thou hast found grace!' And so,
covered with his brothers' kisses, Richard is dragged onto the scaffold,
and led to the guillotine. And they chopped off his head in brotherly
fashion, because he had found grace. Yes, that's characteristic. That pamphlet is translated into Russian by some Russian philanthropists of aris-

tocratic rank and evangelical aspirations, and has been distributed gratis
for the enlightenment of the people. The case of Richard is interesting
because it's national. Though to us it's absurd to cut off a man's head,
because he has become our brother and has found grace, yet we have
our own specialty, which is all but worse. Our historical pastime is the
direct satisfaction of inflicting pain. There are lines in Nekrassov describing how a peasant lashes a horse on the eyes, 'on its meek eyes';
everyone must have seen it. It's peculiarly Russian. He describes how a
feeble little nag had foundered under too heavy a load and cannot move.
The peasant beats it, beats it savagely, beats it at last not knowing what
he is doing in the intoxication of cruelty, thrashes it mercilessly over
and over again. 'However weak you are, you must pull, if you die for it.'
The nag strains, and he begins lashing the poor defenseless creature on
its weeping, on its 'meek eyes.' The frantic beast tugs and draws the
load, trembling all over, gasping for breath, moving sideways, with a sort
of unnatural spasmodic action—it's awful in Nekrassov. But that's only
a horse, and God has given horses to be beaten. So the Tatars have
taught us, and they left us the knout as a rememberance of it. But men,
too, can be beaten. A well-educated, cultured gentleman and his wife
beat their own child with a birchrod, a girl of seven. I have an exact
account of it. The papa was glad that the birch was covered with twigs.
'It stings more,' said he, and so he began stinging his daughter. I know
for a fact there are people who at every blow are worked up to sensuality, to literal sensuality, which increases progressively at every blow
they inflict. They beat for a minute, for five minutes, for ten minutes,
more often and more savagely. The child screams. At last the child
cannot scream, it gasps, 'Daddy! daddy!' By some diabolical unseemly
chance the case was brought into court. A counsel was engaged. The
Russian people have long called a barrister 'a conscience for hire.' The
counsel protests in his client's defense. 'It's such a simple thing,' he
says, 'an everyday domestic event. A father corrects his child. To our
shame be it said, it is brought into court.' The jury, convinced by him,
gives a favorable verdict. The public roars with delight that the torturer
is acquitted. Ah, pity I wasn't there! I would have proposed to raise a
subscription in his honor! . . . Charming pictures.

"But I've still better things about children. I've collected a great,
great deal about Russian children, Alyosha. There was a little girl of

five who was hated by her father and mother, 'most worthy and respectable people, of good education and breeding.' You see, I must repeat again, it is a peculiar characteristic of many people, this love of torturing children, and children only. To all other types of humanity these torturers behave mildly and benevolently like cultivated and humane Europeans; but they are very fond of tormenting children, even fond of children themselves in that sense. It's just their defenselessness that tempts the tormentor, just the angelic confidence of the child who has no refuge and no appeal that sets his vile blood on fire. In every man, of course, a demon lies hidden—the demon of rage, the demon of lustful heat at the screams of the tortured victim, the demon of lawlessness let off the chain, the demon of diseases that follow on vice, gout, kidney disease, and so on.

"This poor child of five was subjected to every possible torture by those cultivated parents. They beat her, thrashed her, kicked her for no reason till her body was one bruise. Then, they went to greater refinements of cruelty—shut her up all night in the cold and frost in a privy, and because she didn't ask to be taken up at night (as though a child of five sleeping its angelic, sound sleep could be trained to wake and ask), they smeared her face and filled her mouth with excrement, and it was her mother, her mother did this. And that mother could sleep, hearing the poor child's groans! Can you understand why a little creature, who can't even understand what's done to her, should beat her little aching heart with her tiny fist in the dark and the cold, and weep her meek unresentful tears to dear, kind God to protect her? Do you understand that, friend and brother, you pious and humble novice? Do you understand why this infamy must be and is permitted? Without it, I am told, man could not have existed on earth, for he could not have known good and evil. Why should he know that diabolical good and evil when it costs so much? Why, the whole world of knowledge is not worth that child's prayer to 'dear, kind God'! I say nothing of the sufferings of grown-up people, they have eaten the apple, damn them, and the devil take them all! But these little ones! I am making you suffer, Alyosha, you are not yourself. I'll leave off it if you like."

"Never mind. I want to suffer too," muttered Alyosha.

"One picture, only one more, because it's so curious, so characteristic, and I have only just read it in some collection of Russian antiquities.

I've forgotten the name. I must look it up. It was in the darkest days of serfdom at the beginning of the century, and long live the Liberator of the People! There was in those days a general of aristocratic connections, the owner of great estates, one of those men—somewhat exceptional, I believe, even then—who, retiring from the service into a life of leisure, are convinced that they've earned absolute power over the lives of the subjects. There were such men then. So our general, settled on his property of two thousand souls, lives in pomp, and domineers over his poor neighbors as though they were dependents and buffoons. He has kennels of hundreds of hounds and nearly a hundred dog-boys—all mounted, and in uniform. One day a serf boy, a little child of eight, threw a stone in play and hurt the paw of the general's favorite hound. 'Why is my favorite dog lame?' He is told that the boy threw a stone that hurt the dog's paw. 'So you did it.' The general looked the child up and down. 'Take him.' He was taken—taken from his mother and kept shut up all night. Early that morning the general comes out on horseback, with the hounds, his dependents, dog-boys, and huntsmen, all mounted around him in full hunting parade. The servants are summoned for their edification, and in front of them all stands the mother of the child. The child is brought from the lockup. It's a gloomy, cold, foggy autumn day, a capital day for hunting. The general orders the child to be undressed; the child is stripped naked. He shivers, numb with terror, not daring to cry . . . 'Make him run,' commands the general. 'Run! run!' shout the dog-boys. The boy runs . . . 'At him!' yells the general, and he sets the whole pack of hounds on the child. The hounds catch him, and tear him to pieces before his mother's eyes! . . . I believe the general was afterwards declared incapable of administering his estates. Well—what did he deserve? To be shot? To be shot for the satisfaction of our moral feelings? Speak, Alyosha!"

"To be shot," murmured Alyosha, lifting his eyes to Ivan with a pale twisted smile.

"Bravo!" cried Ivan delighted. "If even you say so . . . You're a pretty monk! So there is a little devil sitting in your heart, Alyosha Karamazov!"

"What I said was absurd, but——"

"That's just the point that 'but'!" cried Ivan. "Let me tell you, novice, that the absurd is only too necessary on earth. The world stands on absurdities, and perhaps nothing would have come to pass in it without them. We know what we know!"

"What do you know?"

"I understand nothing," Ivan went on, as though in delirium. "I don't want to understand anything now. I want to stick to the fact. I made up my mind long ago not to understand. If I try to understand anything, I shall be false to the fact and I have determined to stick to the fact."

"Why are you trying me?" Alyosha cried, with sudden distress. "Will you say what you mean at last?"

"Of course, I will; that's what I've been leading up to. You are dear to me, I don't want to let you go, and I won't give you up to your Zossima."

Ivan for a minute was silent, his face became all at once very sad.

"Listen! I took the case of children only to make my case clearer. Of the other tears of humanity with which the earth is soaked from its crust to its center, I will say nothing. I have narrowed my subject on purpose, I am a bug, and I recognize in all humility that I cannot understand why the world is arranged as it is. Men are themselves to blame, I suppose; they were given paradise, they wanted freedom, and stole fire from heaven, though they knew they would become unhappy, so there is no need to pity them. With my pitiful, earthly, Euclidean understanding, all I know is that there is suffering and that there are none guilty; that cause follows effect, simply and directly; that everything flows and finds its level—but that's only Euclidean nonsense, I know that, and I can't consent to live by it! What comfort is to me that there are none guilty and that cause follows effect simply and directly, and that I know it—I must have justice, or I will destroy myself. And not justice in some remote infinite time and space, but here on earth, and that I could see myself. I have believed in it. I want to see it, and if I am dead by then, let me rise again, for if it all happens without me, it will be too unfair. Surely I haven't suffered, simply that I, my crimes and my sufferings, may manure the soil of the future harmony for somebody else. I want to see with my own eyes the hind lie down with the lion and the victim rise up and embrace his murderer. I want to be there when everyone suddenly understands what it has all been for. All the religions of the world are built on this longing, and I am a believer. But there are the children, and what am I to do about them? That's a question I can't answer. For the hundredth time I repeat, there are numbers of questions, but I've only taken the children, because in their case what I mean is so unanswerably clear. Listen! If all must suffer to pay for the eternal harmony, what have children to do with it, tell me, please? It's beyond all comprehension why they should suffer, and why they should pay for the harmony. Why should they, too, furnish material to enrich the soil for the harmony of the future? I understand solidarity in sin among men. I understand solidarity in retribution, too; but there can be no such solidarity with children. And if it is really true that they must share responsibility for all their fathers' crimes, such a truth is not of this world and is beyond my comprehension. Some jester will say, perhaps, that the child would have grown up and have sinned, but you see he didn't grow up, he was torn to pieces by the dogs, at eight years old. Oh, Alyosha, I am not blaspheming! I understand, of course, what an upheaval of the universe it will be, when everything in heaven and earth blends in one hymn of praise and everything that lives and has lived cries aloud: 'Thou art just, O Lord, for Thy ways are revealed.' When the mother embraces the fiend who threw her child to the dogs, and all three cry aloud with tears, 'Thou are just, O Lord!' then, of course, the crown of knowledge will be reached and all will be made clear. But what pulls me up here is that I can't accept that harmony. And while I am on earth, I make haste to take my own measures. You see, Alyosha, perhaps it really may happen that if I live to that moment, or rise again to see it, I, too, perhaps, may cry aloud with the rest, looking at the mother embracing the child's torturer, 'Thou are just, O Lord!' but I don't want to cry aloud then. While there is still time, I hasten to protect myself and so I renounce the higher harmony altogether. It's not worth the tears of that one tortured child who beat itself on the breast with its little fist and prayed in its stinking outhouse with an unexpiated tear to 'dear, kind God'! It's not worth it, because those tears are unatoned for. They must be atoned for, or there can be no harmony. But how? How are you going to atone for them? Is it possible? By their being avenged? But what do I care for avenging them? What do I care for a hell for oppressors? What good can hell do, since those children have already been tortured? And what becomes of harmony, if there is hell? I want to forgive. I want to embrace. I don't want more suffering.

And if the sufferings of children go to swell the sum of sufferings which was necessary to pay for truth, then I protest that the truth is not worth such a price. I don't want the mother to embrace the oppressor who threw her son to the dogs! She dare not forgive him! Let her forgive him for herself, if she will, let her forgive the torturer for the immeasurable suffering of her mother's heart. But the sufferings of her tortured child she has no right to forgive; she dare not forgive the torturer, even if the child were to forgive him! And if that is so, if they dare not forgive, what becomes of harmony? Is there in the whole world a being who would have the right to forgive and could forgive? I don't want harmony. From love for humanity I don't want it. I would rather be left with the unavenged suffering. I would rather remain with my unavenged suffering and unsatisfied indignation, *even if I were wrong.* Besides, too high a price is asked for harmony; it's beyond our means to pay so much to enter on it. And so I hasten to give back my entrance ticket, and if I am an honest man I am bound to give it back as soon as possible. And that I am doing. It's not God that I don't accept, Alyosha, only I most respectfully return Him the ticket."

"That's rebellion," murmured Alyosha, looking down.

"Rebellion? I am sorry you call it that," said Ivan earnestly. "One can hardly live in rebellion, and I want to live. Tell me yourself, I challenge you—answer. Imagine that you are creating a fabric of human destiny with the object of making men happy in the end, giving them peace and rest at last, but that it was essential and inevitable to torture to death only one tiny creature—that baby beating its breast with its fist, for instance—and to found that edifice on its unavenged tears, would you consent to be the architect on those conditions? Tell me, and tell the truth."

"No, I wouldn't consent," said Alyosha softly. . . .

DIALOGUES CONCERNING

NATURAL RELIGION

DAVID HUME

PART X

It is my opinion, I own, replied Demea, that each man feels, in a manner, the truth of religion within his own breast, and, from a consciousness of his imbecility and misery rather than from any reasoning, is led to seek protection from that Being on whom he and all nature is dependent. So anxious or so tedious are even the best scenes of life that futurity is still the object of all our hopes and fears. We incessantly look forward and endeavor, by prayers, adoration, and sacrifice, to appease those unknown powers whom we find, by experience, so able to afflict and oppress us. Wretched creatures that we are! What resource for us amidst the innumerable ills of life did not religion suggest some methods of atonement, and appease those terrors with which we are incessantly agitated and tormented?

From Dialogues Concerning Natural Religion, *H. D. Aiken, ed. (New York: Hafner Publishing Co., Inc., 1955). Reprinted by permission of Hafner Publishing Co., Inc.*

I am indeed persuaded, said Philo, that the best and indeed the only method of bringing everyone to a due sense of religion is by just representations of the misery and wickedness of men. And for that purpose a talent of eloquence and strong imagery is more requisite than that of reasoning and argument. For is it necessary to prove what everyone feels within himself? It is only necessary to make us feel it, if possible, more intimately and sensibly.

The people, indeed, replied Demea, are sufficiently convinced of this great and melancholy truth. The miseries of life, the unhappiness of man, the general corruptions of our nature, the unsatisfactory enjoyment of pleasures, riches, honors—these phrases have become almost proverbial in all languages. And who can doubt of what all men declare from their own immediate feeling and experience?

In this point, said Philo, the learned are perfectly agreed with the vulgar; and in all letters, *sacred* and *profane,* the topic of human misery has been insisted on with the most pathetic eloquence that sorrow and melancholy could inspire. The poets, who speak from sentiment, without a system, and whose testimony has therefore the more authority, abound in images of this nature. From Homer down to Dr. Young, the whole inspired tribe have ever been sensible that no other representation of things would suit the feeling and observation of each individual.

As to authorities, replied Demea, you need not seek them. Look round this library of Cleanthes. I shall venture to affirm that, except authors of particular sciences, such as chemistry or botany, who have no occasion to treat of human life, there is scarce one of those innumerable writers from whom the sense of human misery has not, in some passage or other, extorted a complaint and confession of it. At least, the chance is entirely on that side; and no one author has ever, so far as I can recollect, been so extravagant as to deny it.

There you must excuse me, said Philo: Leibniz has denied it, and is perhaps the first[1] who ventured upon so bold and paradoxical an opinion; at least, the first who made it essential to his philosophical system.

And by being the first, replied Demea, might he not have been sensible of his error? For is this a subject in which philosophers can propose to make discoveries especially in so late an age? And can any man hope

---

[1] That sentiment had been maintained by Dr. King and some few others before Leibniz, though by none of so great fame as that German philosopher.

by a simple denial (for the subject scarcely admits of reasoning) to bear down the united testimony of mankind, founded on sense and consciousness?

And why should man, added he, pretend to an exemption from the lot of all other animals? The whole earth, believe me, Philo, is cursed and polluted. A perpetual war is kindled amongst all living creatures. Necessity, hunger, want stimulate the strong and courageous; fear, anxiety, terror agitate the weak and infirm. The first entrance into life gives anguish to the newborn infant and to its wretched parent; weakness, impotence, distress attend each stage of that life, and it is, at last, finished in agony and horror.

Observe, too, says Philo, the curious artifices of nature in order to embitter the life of every living being. The stronger prey upon the weaker and keep them in perpetual terror and anxiety. The weaker, too, in their turn, often prey upon the stronger, and vex and molest them without relaxation. Consider that innumerable race of insects, which either are bred on the body of each animal or, flying about, infix their stings in him. These insects have others still less than themselves which torment them. And thus on each hand, before and behind, above and below, every animal is surrounded with enemies which incessantly seek his misery and destruction.

Man alone, said Demea, seems to be, in part, an exception to this rule. For by combination in society he can easily master lions, tigers, and bears, whose greater strength and agility naturally enable them to prey upon him.

On the contrary, it is here chiefly, cried Philo, that the uniform and equal maxims of nature are most apparent. Man, it is true, can, by combination, surmount all his *real* enemies and become master of the whole animal creation; but does he not immediately raise up to himself *imaginary* enemies, the demons of his fancy, who haunt him with superstitious terrors and blast every enjoyment of life? His pleasure, as he imagines, becomes in their eyes a crime; his food and repose give them umbrage and offense; his very sleep and dreams furnish new materials to anxious fear; and even death, his refuge from every other ill, presents only the dread of endless and innumerable woes. Nor does the wolf molest more the timid flock than superstition does the anxious breast of wretched mortals.

Besides, consider, Demea: This very society by which we surmount those wild beasts, our natural enemies, what new enemies does it not raise to us? What woe and misery does it not occasion? Man is the greatest enemy of man. Oppression, injustice, contempt, contumely, violence, sedition, war, calumny, treachery, fraud—by these they mutually torment each other, and they would soon dissolve that society which they had formed were it not for the dread of still greater ills which must attend their separation.

But though these external insults, said Demea, from animals, from men, from all the elements, which assault us form a frightful catalog of woes, they are nothing in comparison of those which arise within ourselves, from the distempered condition of our mind and body. How many lie under the lingering torment of diseases? Hear the pathetic enumeration of the great poet.

> Intestine stone and ulcer, colic-pangs,
> Demoniac frenzy, moping melancholy,
> And moon-struck madness, pining atrophy,
> Marasmus, and wide-wasting pestilence.
> Dire was the tossing, deep the groans: *Despair*
> Tended the sick, busiest from couch to couch.
> And over them triumphant *Death* his dart
> Shook: but delay'd to strike, though oft invok'd
> With vows, as their chief good and final hope.[2]

The disorders of the mind, continued Demea, though more secret, are not perhaps less dismal and vexatious. Remorse, shame, anguish, rage, disappointment, anxiety, fear, dejection, despair—who has ever passed through life without cruel inroads from these tormentors? How many have scarcely ever felt any better sensations? Labor and poverty, so abhorred by everyone, are the certain lot of the far greater number; and those few privileged persons who enjoy ease and opulence never reach contentment or true felicity. All the goods of life united would not make a very happy man, but all the ills united would make a wretch indeed; and any one of them almost (and who can be free from every one?), nay, often the absence of one good (and who can possess all?) is sufficient to render life ineligible.

Were a stranger to drop on a sudden into this world, I would show him, as a specimen of its ills, a hospital full of diseases, a prison crowded

---

[2] [Milton: *Paradise Lost*, Book XI.]

with malefactors and debtors, a field of battle strewed with carcasses, a fleet foundering in the ocean, a nation languishing under tyranny, famine, or pestilence. To turn the gay side of life to him and give him a notion of its pleasures—whither should I conduct him? To a ball, to an opera, to court? He might justly think that I was only showing him a diversity of distress and sorrow.

There is no evading such striking instances, said Philo, but by apologies which still further aggravate the charge. Why have all men, I ask, in all ages, complained incessantly of the miseries of life? . . . They have no just reason, says one: these complaints proceed only from their discontented, repining, anxious disposition. . . . And can there possibly, I reply, be a more certain foundation of misery than such a wretched temper?

But if they were really as unhappy as they pretend, says my antagonist, why do they remain in life? . . . Not satisfied with life, afraid of death—this is the secret chain, say I, that holds us. We are terrified, not bribed to the continuance of our existence.

It is only a false delicacy, he may insist, which a few refined spirits indulge, and which has spread these complaints among the whole race of mankind. . . . And what is this delicacy, I ask, which you blame? Is it anything but a greater sensibility to all the pleasures and pains of life? And if the man of a delicate, refined temper, by being so much more alive than the rest of the world, is only so much more unhappy, what judgment must we form in general of human life?

Let men remain at rest, says our adversary, and they will be easy. They are willing artificers of their own misery. . . . No! reply I: an anxious languor follows their repose; disappointment, vexation, trouble, their activity and ambition.

I can observe something like what you mention in some others, replied Cleanthes, but I confess I feel little or nothing of it in myself, and hope that it is not so common as you represent it.

If you feel not human misery yourself, cried Demea, I congratulate you on so happy a singularity. Others, seemingly the most prosperous, have not been ashamed to vent their complaints in the most melancholy strains. Let us attend to the great, the fortunate·emperor, Charles V, when, tired with human grandeur, he resigned all his extensive dominions into the hands of his son. In the last harangue which he made on

that memorable occasion, he publicly avowed *that the greatest prosperi-*
ties which he had ever enjoyed had been mixed with so many adversities
that he might truly say he had never enjoyed any satisfaction or content-
ment. But did the retired life in which he sought for shelter afford him
any greater happiness? If we may credit his son's account, his repentance
commenced the very day of his resignation.

Cicero's fortune, from small beginnings, rose to the greatest luster
and renown; yet what pathetic complaints of the ills of life do his famil-
iar letters, as well as philosophical discourses, contain? And suitably to
his own experience, he introduces Cato, the great, the fortunate Cato
protesting in his old age that had he a new life in his offer he would
reject the present.

Ask yourself, ask any of your acquaintance, whether they would live
over again the last ten or twenty years of their life. No! but the next
twenty, they say, will be better:

> And from the dregs of life, hope to receive
> What the first sprightly running could not give.[3]

Thus, at last, they find (such is the greatness of human misery, it rec-
onciles even contradictions) that they complain at once of the shortness
of life and of its vanity and sorrow.

And is it possible, Cleanthes, said Philo, that after all these reflections,
and infinitely more which might be suggested, you can still persevere in
your anthropomorphism, and assert the moral attributes of the Deity,
his justice, benevolence, mercy, and rectitude, to be of the same nature
with these virtues in human creatures? His power, we allow, is infinite;
whatever he wills is executed; but neither man nor any other animal is
happy; therefore, he does not will their happiness. His wisdom is infinite;
he is never mistaken in choosing the means to any end; but the course
of nature tends not to human or animal felicity; therefore, it is not established for that purpose. Through the whole compass of human knowledge
there are no inferences more certain and infallible than these. In what
respect, then, do his benevolence and mercy resemble the benevolence and
mercy of men?

Epicurus' old questions are yet unanswered.

Is he willing to prevent evil, but not able? then is he impotent. Is he

---

[3] [John Dryden, *Aureng-Zebe,* Act IV, Scene 1.]

able, but not willing? then is he malevolent. Is he both able and willing? whence then is evil?

You ascribe, Cleanthes, (and I believe justly) a purpose and intention to nature. But what, I beseech you, is the object of that curious artifice and machinery which she has displayed in all animals—the preservation alone of individuals, and propagation of the species? It seems enough for her purpose, if such a rank be barely upheld in the universe, without any care or concern for the happiness of the members that compose it. No resource for this purpose: no machinery in order merely to give pleasure or ease; no fund of pure joy and contentment; no indulgence without some want or necessity accompanying it. At least, the few phenomena of this nature are overbalanced by opposite phenomena of still greater importance.

Our sense of music, harmony, and indeed beauty of all kinds, gives satisfaction, without being absolutely necessary to the preservation and propagation of the species. But what racking pains, on the other hand, arise from gouts, gravels, megrims, toothaches, rheumatisms, where the injury to the animal machinery is either small or incurable? Mirth, laughter, play, frolic seem gratuitous satisfactions which have no further tendency; spleen, melancholy, discontent, superstition are pains of the same nature. How then does the Divine benevolence display itself, in the sense of you anthropomorphites? None but we mystics, as you were pleased to call us, can account for this strange mixture of phenomena, by deriving it from attributes infinitely perfect but incomprehensible.

And have you, at last, said Cleanthes smiling, betrayed your intentions, Philo? Your long agreement with Demea did indeed a little surprise me, but I find you were all the while erecting a concealed battery against me. And I must confess that you have now fallen upon a subject worthy of your noble spirit of opposition and controversy. If you can make out the present point, and prove mankind to be unhappy or corrupted, there is an end at once of all religion. For to what purpose establish the natural attributes of the Deity, while the moral are still doubtful and uncertain?

You take umbrage very easily, replied Demea, at opinions the most innocent and the most generally received, even amongst the religious and devout themselves; and nothing can be more surprising than to find a topic like this—concerning the wickedness and misery of man—charged with no less than atheism and profaneness. Have not all pious divines and preachers who have indulged their rhetoric on so fertile a subject, have they not easily, I say, given a solution of any difficulties which may attend it? This world is but a point in comparison of the universe; this life but a moment in comparison of eternity. The present evil phenomena, therefore, are rectified in other regions, and in some future period of existence. And the eyes of men, being then opened to larger views of things, see the whole connection of general laws, and trace, with adoration, the benevolence and rectitude of the Deity through all the mazes and intricacies of his providence.

No! replied Cleanthes, no! These arbitrary suppositions can never be admitted, contrary to matter of fact, visible and uncontroverted. Whence can any cause be known but from its known effects? Whence can any hypothesis be proved but from the apparent phenomena? To establish one hypothesis upon another is building entirely in the air; and the utmost we ever attain by these conjectures and fictions is to ascertain the bare possibility of our opinion, but never can we, upon such terms, establish its reality.

The only method of supporting Divine benevolence—and it is what 1 willingly embrace—is to deny absolutely the misery and wickedness of man. Your representations are exaggerated; your melancholy views mostly fictitious; your inferences contrary to fact and experience. Health is more common than sickness; pleasure than pain; happiness than misery. And for one vexation which we meet with, we attain, upon computation, a hundred enjoyments.

Admitting your position, replied Philo, which yet is extremely doubtful, you must at the same time allow that, if pain be less frequent than pleasure, it is infinitely more violent and durable. One hour of it is often able to outweigh a day, a week, a month of our common insipid enjoyments; and how many days, weeks, and months are passed by several in the most acute torments? Pleasure, scarcely in one instance, is ever able to reach ecstasy and rapture; and in no one instance can it continue for any time at its highest pitch and altitude. The spirits evaporate, the nerves relax, the fabric is disordered, and the enjoyment quickly degenerates into fatigue and uneasiness. But pain often, good God, how often! rises to torture and agony; and the longer it continues, it becomes still more genuine agony and torture. Patience is exhausted, courage languishes, melancholy seizes us, and nothing terminates our misery but the removal of its cause or another event which is the sole cure of all evil, but which, from our natural folly, we regard with still greater horror and consternation.

But not to insist upon these topics, continued Philo, though most obvious, certain, and important, I must use the freedom to admonish you, Cleanthes, that you have put the controversy upon a most dangerous issue, and are unawares introducing a total skepticism into the most essential articles of natural and revealed theology. What! no method of fixing a just foundation for religion unless we allow the happiness of human life, and maintain a continued existence even in this world, with all our present pains, infirmities, vexations, and follies, to be eligible and desirable! But this is contrary to everyone's feeling and experience; it is contrary to an authority so established as nothing can subvert. No decisive proofs can ever be produced against this authority; nor is it possible for you to compute, estimate, and compare all the pains and all the pleasures in the lives of all men and of all animals; and thus, by your resting the whole system of religion on a point which, from its very nature, must forever be uncertain, you tacitly confess that that system is equally uncertain.

But allowing you what never will be believed, at least, what you never possibly can prove, that animal or, at least, human happiness in this life exceeds its misery, you have yet done nothing; for this is not, by any means, what we expect from infinite power, infinite wisdom, and infinite goodness. Why is there any misery at all in the world? Not by chance, surely. From some cause then. Is it from the intention of the Deity? But he is perfectly benevolent. Is it contrary to his intention? But he is almighty. Nothing can shake the solidity of this reasoning, so short, so clear, so decisive, except we assert that these subjects exceed all human capacity, and that our common measures of truth and falsehood are not applicable to them—a topic which I have all along insisted on, but which you have, from the beginning, rejected with scorn and indignation.

But I will be contented to retire still from this entrenchment, for I deny that you can ever force me in it. I will allow that pain or misery in man is *compatible* with infinite power and goodness in the Deity, even in your sense of these attributes: what are you advanced by all these concessions? A mere possible compatibility is not sufficient. You must *prove* these pure, unmixed, and uncontrollable attributes from the present mixed and confused phenomena, and from these alone. A hopeful undertaking! Were the phenomena ever so pure and unmixed, yet, being finite, they would be insufficient for that purpose. How much more, where they are also so jarring and discordant!

Here, Cleanthes, I find myself at ease in my argument. Here I triumph. Formerly, when we argued concerning the natural attributes of intelligence and design, I needed all my skeptical and metaphysical subtlety to elude your grasp. In many views of the universe and of its parts, particularly the latter, the beauty and fitness of final causes strike us with such irresistible force that all objections appear (what I believe they really are) mere cavils and sophisms; nor can we then imagine how it was ever possible for us to repose any weight on them. But there is no view of human life or of the condition of mankind from which, without the greatest violence, we can infer the moral attributes or learn that infinite benevolence, conjoined with infinite power and infinite wisdom, which we must discover by the eyes of faith alone. It is your turn now to tug the laboring oar, and to support your philosophical subtleties against the dictates of plain reason and experience.

PART XI

I scruple not to allow, said Cleanthes, that I have been apt to suspect the frequent repetition of the word *infinite,* which we meet with in all theological writers, to savor more of panegyric than of philosophy, and that any purposes of reasoning, and even of religion, would be better served were we to rest contented with more accurate and more moderate expressions. The terms *admirable, excellent, superlatively great, wise,* and *holy*—these sufficiently fill the imaginations of men, and anything beyond, besides that it leads into absurdities, has no influence on the affections or sentiments. Thus, in the present subject, if we abandon all human analogy, as seems your intention, Demea, I am afraid we abandon all religion and retain no conception of the great object of our adoration. If we preserve human analogy, we must forever find it impossible to reconcile any mixture of evil in the universe with infinite attributes; much less can we ever prove the latter from the former. But supposing the Author of nature to be finitely perfect, though far exceeding mankind, a satisfactory account may then be given of natural and moral evil, and every untoward phenomenon be explained and adjusted. A less evil may then be chosen in order to avoid a greater; inconveniences be submitted to in order to reach a desirable end; and, in a word, benevolence, regulated by wisdom and limited by necessity, may produce just such a world as the present. You, Philo, who are so prompt at starting views and reflections and analogies, I would gladly hear, at length, without interruption, your opinion of this new theory; and if it deserve our attention, we may afterwards, at more leisure, reduce it into form.

My sentiments, replied Philo, are not worth being made a mystery of; and, therefore, without any ceremony, I shall deliver what occurs to me with regard to the present subject. It must, I think, be allowed that, if a very limited intelligence whom we shall suppose utterly unacquainted with the universe were assured that it were the production of a very good, wise, and powerful Being, however finite, he would, from his conjectures, form *beforehand* a different notion of it from what we find it to be by experience; nor would he ever imagine, merely from these attributes of the cause of which he is informed, that the effect could be so full of vice and misery and disorder, as it appears in this life. Supposing now that this person were brought into the world, still assured that it was the workmanship of such a sublime and benevolent Being, he might, perhaps, be surprised at the disappointment, but would never retract his former belief if founded on any very solid argument, since such a limited intelligence must be sensible of his own blandness and ignorance, and must allow that there may be many solutions of those phenomena which will forever escape his comprehension. But supposing, which is the real case with regard to man, that this creature is not antecedently convinced of a supreme intelligence, benevolent, and powerful, but is left to gather such a belief from the appearances of things—this entirely alters the case, nor will he ever find any reason for such a conclusion. He may be fully convinced of the narrow limits of his understanding, but this will not help him in forming an inference concerning the goodness of superior powers, since he must form that inference from what he knows, not from what he is ignorant of. The more you exaggerate his weakness and ignorance, the more diffident you render him, and give him the greater suspicion that such subjects are beyond the reach of his faculties. You are obliged, therefore, to reason with him merely from the known phenomena, and to drop every arbitrary supposition or conjecture.

Did I show you a house or palace where there was not one apartment convenient or agreeable, where the windows, doors, fires, passages, stairs, and the whole economy of the building were the source of noise, confusion, fatigue, darkness, and the extremes of heat and cold, you would certainly blame the contrivance, without any further examination. The architect would in vain display his subtlety, and prove to you that, if this door or that window were altered, greater ills would ensue. What he says may be strictly true: the alteration of one particular, while the other parts of the building remain, may only augment the inconveniences. But still you would assert in general that, if the architect had had skill and good intentions, he might have formed such a plan of the whole, and might have adjusted the parts in such a manner as would have remedied all or most of these inconveniences. His ignorance, or even your own ignorance of such a plan, will never convince you of the impossibility of it. If you find any inconveniences and deformities in the building, you will always, without entering into any detail, condemn the architect.

In short, I repeat the question: Is the world, considered in general and as it appears to us in this life, different from what a man or such a limited being would, *beforehand,* expect from a very powerful, wise, and benevolent Deity? It must be strange prejudice to assert the contrary. And from thence I conclude that, however consistent the world may be, allowing certain suppositions and conjectures with the idea of such a Deity, it can never afford us an inference concerning his existence. The consistency is not absolutely denied, only the inference. Conjectures, especially where infinity is excluded from the Divine attributes, may perhaps be sufficient to prove a consistency, but can never be foundations for any inference.

There seem to be *four* circumstances on which depend all or the greatest part of the ills that molest sensible creatures; and it is not impossible but all these circumstances may be necessary and unavoidable. We know so little beyond common life, or even of common life, that, with regard to the economy of a universe, there is no conjecture, however wild, which may not be just, nor any one, however plausible, which may not be erroneous. All that belongs to human understanding, in this deep ignorance and obscurity, is to be skeptical or at least cautious, and not to admit of any hypothesis whatever, much less of any which is supported by no appearance of probability. Now this I assert to be the case with regard to all the causes of evil and the circumstances on which it depends. None of them appear to human reason in the least degree necessary or unavoidable, nor can we suppose them such, without the utmost license of imagination.

The *first* circumstance which introduces evil is that contrivance or economy of the animal creation by which pains, as well as pleasures, are employed to excite all creatures to action, and make them vigilant in the great work of self-preservation. Now pleasure alone, in its various degrees, seems to human understanding sufficient for this purpose. All animals might be constantly in a state of enjoyment; but when urged by any of the necessities of nature, such as thirst, hunger, weariness, instead of pain, they might feel a diminution of pleasure by which they might be prompted to seek that object which is necessary to their subsistence. Men pursue pleasure as eagerly as they avoid pain; at least, they might have been so constituted. It seems, therefore, plainly possible to carry on the business of life without any pain. Why then is any animal ever rendered susceptible of such a sensation? If animals can be free from it an hour, they might enjoy a perpetual exemption from it, and it required as particular a contrivance of their organs to produce that feeling as to endow them with sight, hearing, or any of the senses. Shall we conjecture that such a contrivance was necessary, without any appearance of reason, and shall we build on that conjecture as on the most certain truth?

But a capacity of pain would not alone produce pain were it not for the *second* circumstance, viz., the conducting of the world by general laws; and this seems nowise necessary to a very perfect Being. It is true, if everything were conducted by particular volitions, the course of nature would be perpetually broken, and no man could employ his reason in the conduct of life. But might not other particular volitions remedy this inconvenience? In short, might not the Deity exterminate all ill, wherever it were to be found, and produce all good, without any preparation or long progress of causes and effects?

Besides, we must consider that, according to the present economy of the world, the course of nature, though supposed exactly regular, yet to us appears not so, and many events are uncertain, and many disappoint our expectations. Health and sickness, calm and tempest, with an infinite number of other accidents whose causes are unknown and variable, have a great influence both on the fortunes of particular persons and on the prosperity of public societies; and indeed all human life, in a manner, depends on such accidents. A being, therefore, who knows the secret springs of the universe might easily, by particular volitions, turn all these accidents to the good of mankind and render the whole world happy, without discovering himself in any operation. A fleet whose purposes were salutary to society might always meet with a fair wind. Good princes enjoy sound health and long life. Persons born to power and authority be framed with good tempers and virtuous dispositions. A few such events as these, regularly and wisely conducted, would change the face of the world, and yet would no more seem to disturb the course of nature or confound human conduct than the present economy of things where the causes are secret and variable and compounded. Some small touches given to Caligula's brain in his infancy might have converted him into a Trajan. One wave, a little higher than the rest, by burying Caesar and his fortune in the bottom of the ocean, might have restored liberty to a considerable part of mankind. There may, for aught we know, be good reasons why Providence interposes not in this manner, but they are unknown to us; and, though the mere supposition that such reasons exist may be sufficient to *save* the conclusion concerning the Divine attributes, yet surely it can never be sufficient to *establish* that conclusion.

If everything in the universe be conducted by general laws, and if animals be rendered susceptible of pain, it scarcely seems possible but some ill must arise in the various shocks of matter and the various concurrence and opposition of general laws; but this ill would be very rare were it not for the *third* circumstance which I proposed to mention, viz., the great frugality with which all powers and faculties are distributed to every particular being. So well adjusted are the organs and capacities of all animals, and so well fitted to their preservation, that, as far as history or tradition reaches, there appears not to be any single species which has yet been extinguished in the universe. Every animal has the requisite endowments, but these endowments are bestowed with so scrupulous an economy that any considerable diminution must entirely destroy the creature. Wherever one power is increased, there is a proportional abatement in the others. Animals which excel in swiftness are commonly defective in force. Those which possess both are either imperfect in some of their senses or are oppressed with the most craving wants. The human species, whose chief excellence is reason and sagacity, is of all others the most necessitous, and the most deficient in bodily advantages, without clothes, without arms, without food, without lodging, without any convenience of life, except what they owe to their own skill and industry. In short, nature seems to have formed an exact calculation of the necessities of her creatures, and, like a *rigid master,* has afforded them little more powers or endowments than what are strictly sufficient to supply those necessities. An *indulgent parent* would have bestowed a large stock in order to guard against accidents, and secure the happiness and welfare of the creature in the most unfortunate concurrence of circumstances. Every course of life would not have been so surrounded with precipices that the least departure from the true path, by mistake or necessity, must involve us in misery and ruin. Some reserve, some fund, would have been provided to ensure happiness, nor would the powers and the necessities have been adjusted with so rigid an economy. The Author of nature is inconceivably powerful; his force is supposed great, if not altogether inexhaustible, nor is there any reason, as far as we can judge, to make him observe this strict frugality in his dealings with his creatures. It would have been better, were his power extremely limited, to have created fewer animals, and to have endowed these with more faculties for their happiness and preservation. A builder is never esteemed prudent who undertakes a plan beyond what his stock will enable him to finish.

In order to cure most of the ills of human life, I require not that man should have the wings of the eagle, the swiftness of the stag, the force of the ox, the arms of the lion, the scales of the crocodile or rhinoceros; much less do I demand the sagacity of an angel or cherubim. I am contented to take an increase in one single power or faculty of his soul. Let him be endowed with a greater propensity to industry and labor, a more vigorous spring and activity of mind, a more constant bent to business and application. Let the whole species possess naturally an equal diligence with that which many individuals are able to attain by habit and reflection, and the most beneficial consequences, without any allay of ill, is the immediate and necessary result of this endowment. Almost all the moral as well as natural evils of human life arise from idleness; and were our species, by the original constitution of their frame, exempt from this vice or infirmity, the perfect cultivation of land, the improvement of arts and manufactures, the exact execution of every office and duty, immediately follow; and men at once may fully reach that state of society which is so imperfectly attained by the best-regulated government. But as industry is a power, and the most valuable of any, nature seems determined, suitably to her usual maxims, to bestow it on men with a very sparing hand, and rather to punish him severely for his deficiency in it than to reward him for his attainments. She has so contrived his frame that nothing but the most violent necessity can oblige him to labor; and she employs all his other wants to overcome, at least in part, the want of diligence, and to endow him with some share of a faculty of which she has thought fit naturally to bereave him. Here our demands may be allowed very humble, and therefore the more reasonable. If we required the endowments of superior penetration and judgment, of a more delicate taste of beauty, of a nicer sensibility to benevolence and friendship, we might be told that we impiously pretend to break the order of nature, that we want to exalt ourselves into a higher rank of being, that the presents which we require, not being suitable to our state and condition, would only be pernicious to us. But it is hard, I dare to repeat it, it is hard that, being placed in a world so full of wants and necessities, where almost every being and element is either our foe or refuses its assistance . . . we should also have our own temper to struggle with, and should be deprived of that faculty which can alone fence against these multiplied evils.

The *fourth* circumstance whence arises the misery and ill of the universe is the inaccurate workmanship of all the springs and principles of the great machine of nature. It must be acknowledged that there are few parts of the universe which seem not to serve some purpose, and whose removal would not produce a visible defect and disorder in the whole. The parts hang all together, nor can one be touched without affecting the rest, in a greater or less degree. But at the same time, it must be observed that none of these parts or principles, however useful, are so accurately adjusted as to keep precisely within those bounds in which their utility consists; but they are, all of them, apt, on every occasion, to run into the one extreme or the other. One would imagine that this grand production had not received the last hand of the maker—so little finished is every part, and so coarse are the strokes with which it is executed. Thus the winds are requisite to convey the vapors along the surface of the globe, and to assist men in navigation; but how often, rising up to tempests and hurricanes, do they become pernicious? Rains are necessary to nourish all the plants and animals of the earth; but how often are they defective? how often excessive? Heat is requisite to all life and vegetation, but is not always found in the due proportion. On the mixture and secretion of the humors and juices of the body depend the health and prosperity of the animal; but the parts perform not regularly their proper function. What more useful than all the passions of the mind, ambition, vanity, love, anger? But how often do they break their bounds and cause the greatest convulsions in society? There is nothing so advantageous in the universe but what frequently becomes pernicious, by its excess or defect; nor has nature guarded, with the requisite accuracy, against all disorder or confusion. The irregularity is never perhaps so great as to destroy any species, but is often sufficient to involve the individuals in ruin and misery.

On the concurrence, then, of these *four* circumstances does all or the greatest part of natural evil depend. Were all living creatures incapable of pain, or were the world administered by particular volitions, evil never could have found access into the universe; and were animals endowed with a large stock of powers and faculties, beyond what strict necessity requires, or were the several springs and principles of the universe so accurately framed as to preserve always the just temperament and medium, there must have been very little ill in comparison with what we feel at present. What then shall we pronounce on this occasion? Shall we say that these circumstances are not necessary, and they might easily have been altered in the contrivance of the universe? This decision seems too presumptuous for creatures so blind and ignorant. Let us be more modest in our conclusions. Let us allow that, if the goodness of the Deity (I mean a goodness like the human) could be established on any tolerable reasons a priori, these phenomena however untoward, would not be sufficient to subvert that principle, but might easily, in some unknown manner, be reconcilable to it. But let us still assert that, as this goodness is not antecedently established but must be inferred from the phenomena, there can be no grounds for such an inference while there are so many ills in the universe, and while these ills might so easily have been remedied, as far as human understanding can be allowed to judge on such a subject. I am skeptic enough to allow that the bad appearances, notwithstanding all my reasonings, may be compatible with such attributes as you suppose, but surely they can never prove these attributes. Such a conclusion cannot result from skepticism, but must arise from the phenomena, and from our confidence in the reasonings which we deduce from these phenomena.

Look round this universe. What an immense profusion of beings, animated and organized, sensible and active! You admire this prodigious variety and fecundity. But inspect a little more narrowly these living existences, the only beings worth regarding. How hostile and destructive to each other! How insufficient all of them for their own happiness! How contemptible or odious to the spectator! The whole presents nothing but the idea of a blind nature, impregnated by a great vivifying principle, and pouring forth from her lap, without discernment or parental care, her maimed and abortive children!

Here the Manichean system occurs as a proper hypothesis to solve the difficulty; and, no doubt, in some respects it is very specious and has more probability than the common hypothesis, by giving a plausible account of the strange mixture of good and ill which appears in life. But if we consider, on the other hand, the perfect uniformity and agreement of the parts of the universe, we shall not discover in it any marks of the combat of a malevolent with a benevolent being. There is indeed an opposition of pains and pleasures in the feelings of sensible creatures; but are not all the operations of nature carried on by an opposition of principles, of hot and cold, moist and dry, light and heavy? The true conclusion is that the original Source of all things is entirely indifferent to all these principles, and has no more regard to good above ill than to heat above cold, or to drought above moisture, or to light above heavy.

There may *four* hypotheses be framed concerning the first causes of the universe: that they are endowed with perfect goodness; that they have perfect malice; that they are opposite and have both goodness and malice; that they have neither goodness nor malice. Mixed phenomena can never prove the two former unmixed principles; and the uniformity and steadiness of general laws seem to oppose the third. The fourth, therefore, seems by far the most probable.

What I have said concerning natural evil will apply to moral [evil] with little or no variation; and we have no more reason to infer that the rectitude of the Supreme Being resembles human rectitude than that his benevolence resembles the human. Nay, it will be thought that we have still greater cause to exclude from him moral sentiments, such as we feel them, since moral evil, in the opinion of many, is much more predominant above moral good than natural evil above natural good.

But even though this should not be allowed, and though the virtue which is in mankind should be acknowledged much superior to the vice, yet, so long as there is any vice at all in the universe, it will very much puzzle you anthropomorphites how to account for it. You must assign a cause for it, without having recourse to the first cause. But as every effect must have a cause, and that cause another, you must either carry on the progression *in infinitum* or rest on that original principle, who is the ultimate cause of all things. . . .

Hold! hold! cried Demea: Whither does your imagination hurry you? I joined in alliance with you in order to prove the incomprehensible nature of the Divine Being, and refute the principles of Cleanthes, who would measure everything by human rule and standard. But I now find you running into all the topics of the greatest libertines and infidels, and betraying that holy cause which you seemingly espoused. Are you secretly, then, a more dangerous enemy than Cleanthes himself?

And are you so late in perceiving it? replied Cleanthes. Believe me, Demea, your friend Philo, from the beginning, has been amusing himself at both our expense; and it must be confessed that the injudicious reasoning of our vulgar theology has given him but too just a handle of ridicule. The total infirmity of human reason, the absolute incomprehensibility of the Divine Nature, the great and universal misery, and still greater wickedness of men—these are strange topics, surely, to be so fondly cherished by orthodox divines and doctors. In ages of stupidity and ignorance, indeed, these principles may safely be espoused; and perhaps no views of things are more proper to promote superstition than such as encourage the blind amazement, the diffidence, and melancholy of mankind. But at present . . .

Blame not so much, interposed Philo, the ignorance of these reverend gentlemen. They know how to change their style with the times. Formerly, it was a most popular theological topic to maintain that human life was vanity and misery, and to exaggerate all the ills and pains which are incident to men. But of late years, divines, we find, begin to retract this position and maintain, though still with some hesitation, that there are more goods than evils, more pleasures than pains, even in this life. When religion stood entirely upon temper and education, it was thought proper to encourage melancholy, as, indeed, mankind never have recourse to superior powers so readily as in that disposition. But as men have now learned to form principles and to draw consequences, it is necessary to change the batteries, and to make use of such arguments as will endure at least some scrutiny and examination. This variation is the same (and from the same causes) with that which I formerly remarked with regard to skepticism.

Thus Philo continued to the last his spirit of opposition, and his censure of established opinions. But I could observe that Demea did not at all relish the latter part of the discourse; and he took occasion soon after, on some pretense or other, to leave the company.

MR. MANSEL ON

THE LIMITS OF

RELIGIOUS THOUGHT

JOHN STUART MILL

Mr. Mansel may be affirmed, by a fair application of the term, to be, in metaphysics, a pupil of Sir W. Hamilton. I do not mean that he agrees with him in all his opinions; for he avowedly dissents from the peculiar Hamiltonian theory of Cause: still less that he has learnt nothing from any other teacher, or from his own independent speculations. On the contrary, he has shown considerable power of original thought, both of a good and of what seems to me a bad quality. But he is the admiring editor of Sir W. Hamilton's Lectures; he invariably speaks of him with a deference which he pays to no other philosopher; he expressly accepts, in language identical with Sir W. Hamilton's own, the doctrines regarded as specially characteristic of the Hamiltonian philosophy, and may with reason be considered as a representative

From An Examination of Sir William Hamilton's Philosophy, *Chap. 7, "The Philosophy of the Conditioned as Applied by Mr. Mansel to the Limits of Religious Thought" (London: Longmans, Green & Company, Ltd., 1865).*

of the same general mode of thought. Mr. Mansel has bestowed especial cultivation upon a province but slightly touched by his master— the application of the Philosophy of the Conditioned to the theological department of thought; the deduction of such of its corollaries and consequences as directly concern religion.

The premises from which Mr. Mansel reasons are those of Sir W. Hamilton. He maintains the necessary relativity of all our knowledge. He holds that the Absolute and the Infinite, or, to use a more significant expression, an Absolute and an Infinite being, are inconceivable by us; and that when we strive to conceive what is thus inaccessible to our faculties, we fall into self-contradiction. That we are, nevertheless, warranted in believing, and bound to believe, the real existence of an absolute and infinite being, and that this being is God. God, therefore, is inconceivable and unknowable by us, and cannot even be thought of without self-contradiction; that is (for Mr. Mansel is careful thus to qualify the assertion), thought of *as* Absolute, and *as* Infinite. Through this inherent impossibility of our conceiving or knowing God's essential attributes, we are disqualified from judging what is or is not consistent with them. If, then, a religion is presented to us, containing any particular doctrine respecting the Deity, our belief or rejection of the doctrine ought to depend exclusively upon the evidences which can be produced for the divine origin of the religion: and no argument grounded on the incredibility of the doctrine, as involving an intellectual absurdity, or on its moral badness as unworthy of a good or wise being, ought to have any weight, since of these things we are incompetent to judge. This, at least, is the drift of Mr. Mansel's argument: but I am bound to admit that he affirms the conclusion with a certain limitation; for he acknowledges, that the moral character of the doctrines of a religion ought to count for something among the reasons for accepting or rejecting, as of divine origin, the religion as a whole. That it ought also to count for something in the interpretation of the religion when accepted, he neglects to say; but we must in fairness suppose that he would admit it. These concessions, however, to the moral feelings of mankind, are made at the expense of Mr. Mansel's logic. If his theory is correct, he has no right to make either of them.

There is nothing new in this line of argument as applied to theology.

That we cannot understand God; that his ways are not our ways; that we cannot scrutinize or judge his counsels—propositions which, in a reasonable sense of the terms, could not be denied by any Theist—have often before been tendered as reasons why we may assert any absurdities and any moral monstrosities concerning God, and miscall them Goodness and Wisdom. The novelty is in presenting this conclusion as a corollary from the most advanced doctrines of modern philosophy— from the true theory of the powers and limitations of the human mind, on religious and on all other subjects.

My opinion of this doctrine, in whatever way presented, is, that it is simply the most morally pernicious doctrine now current; and that the question it involves is, beyond all others which now engage speculative minds, the decisive one between moral good and evil for the Christian world. It is a momentous matter, therefore, to consider whether we are obliged to adopt it. Without holding Mr. Mansel accountable for the moral consequences of the doctrine, further than he himself accepts them, I think it supremely important to examine whether the doctrine itself is really the verdict of a sound metaphysic; and essential to a true estimation of Sir W. Hamilton's philosophy to enquire whether the conclusion thus drawn from his principal doctrine is justly affiliated on it. I think it will appear that the conclusion not only does not follow from a true theory of the human faculties, but is not even correctly drawn from the premises from which Mr. Mansel infers it. . . .

The fundamental property of our knowledge of God, Mr. Mansel says, is that we do not and cannot know him as he is in himself: certain persons, therefore, whom he calls Rationalists, he condemns as unphilosophical when they reject any statement as inconsistent with the character of God. This is a valid answer, as far as words go, to some of the later Transcendentalists—to those who think that we have an intuition of the Divine Nature; though even as to them it would not be difficult to show that the answer is but skin-deep. But those "Rationalists" who hold, with Mr. Mansel himself, the relativity of human knowledge, are not touched by his reasoning. We cannot know God as he is in himself (they reply); granted: and what then? Can we know man as he is in himself, or matter as it is in itself?

We do not claim any other knowledge of God than such as we have of man or of matter. Because I do not know my fellow-men, nor any of the powers of nature, as they are in themselves, am I therefore not at liberty to disbelieve anything I hear respecting them as being inconsistent with their character? I know something of Man and Nature, not as they are in themselves, but as they are relatively to us; and it is as relative to us, and not as he is in himself, that I suppose myself to know anything of God. The attributes which I ascribe to him, as goodness, knowledge, power, are all relative. They are attributes (says the rationalist) which my experience enables me to conceive, and which I consider as proved, not absolutely, by an intuition of God, but phenomenally, by his action on the creation, as known through my senses and my rational faculty. These relative attributes, each of them in an infinite degree, are all I pretend to predicate of God. When I reject a doctrine as inconsistent with God's nature, it is not as being inconsistent with what God is in himself, but with what he is as manifested to us. If my knowledge of him is only phenomenal, the assertions which I reject are phenomenal too. If those assertions are inconsistent with my relative knowledge of him, it is no answer to say that all my knowledge of him is relative. That is no more a reason against disbelieving an alleged fact as unworthy of God, than against disbelieving another alleged fact as unworthy of Turgot, or of Washington, whom also I do not know as Noumena, but only as Phenomena.

There is but one way for Mr. Mansel out of this difficulty, and he adopts it. He must maintain, not merely that an Absolute Being is unknowable in himself, but that the Relative attributes of an Absolute Being are unknowable likewise. He must say that we do not know what Wisdom, Justice, Benevolence, Mercy are, as they exist in God. Accordingly he does say so. The following are his direct utterances on the subject: as an implied doctrine, it pervades his whole argument.

> It is a fact which experience forces upon us, and which it is useless, were it possible, to disguise, that the representation of God after the model of the highest human morality which we are capable of conceiving, is not sufficient to account for all the phenomena exhibited by the course of his natural Providence. The infliction of physical suffering, the permission of moral evil, the adversity of the good, the prosperity of the wicked, the crimes of the guilty involving the misery of the innocent, the tardy appearance and partial dis-

tribution of moral and religious knowledge in the world—these are
facts which no doubt are reconcilable, we know not how, with the
Infinite Goodness of God, but which certainly are not to be explained on the supposition that its sole and sufficient type is to be
found in the finite goodness of man.[1]

In other words, it is necessary to suppose that the infinite goodness
ascribed to God is not the goodness which we know and love in our
fellow-creatures, distinguished only as infinite in degree, but is different
in kind, and another quality altogether. When we call the one finite
goodness and the other infinite goodness, we do not mean what the words
assert, but something else: we intentionally apply the same name to
things which we regard as different.

Accordingly Mr. Mansel combats, as a heresy of his opponents, the
opinion that infinite goodness differs only in degree from finite goodness.
The notion

that the attributes of God differ from those of man in degree only,
not in kind, and hence that certain mental and moral qualities of
which we are immediately conscious in ourselves, furnish at the same
time a true and adequate image of the infinite perfections of God [2]

(the word *adequate* must have slipped in by inadvertence, since otherwise it would be inexcusable misrepresentation) he identifies with "the
vulgar Rationalism which regards the reason of man, in its ordinary
and normal operation, as the supreme criterion of religious truth." And
in characterizing the mode of arguing of this vulgar Rationalism, he
declares its principles to be, that

all the excellences of which we are conscious in the creature, must
necessarily exist in the same manner, though in a higher degree, in
the Creator. God is indeed more wise, more just, more merciful,
than man; but for that very reason, his wisdom and justice and
mercy, must contain nothing that is incompatible with the corresponding attributes in their human character.[3]

It is against this doctrine that Mr. Mansel feels called on to make
an emphatic protest.

Here, then, I take my stand on the acknowledged principle of logic
and of mortality, that when we mean different things we have no

---

[1] *Limits of Religious Thought,* preface to the fourth edition, p. 13.
[2] *Ibid.,* p. 26.
[3] *Ibid.,* p. 28.

right to call them by the same name, and to apply to them the same
predicates, moral and intellectual. Language has no meaning for the
words Just, Merciful, Benevolent, save that in which we predicate
them of our fellow-creatures; and unless that is what we intend to
express by them, we have no business to employ the words. If in affirming them of God we do not mean to affirm these very qualities, differing
only as greater in degree, we are neither philosophically nor morally
entitled to affirm them at all. If it be said that the qualities are the
same, but that we cannot conceive them as they are when raised to
the infinite, I grant that we cannot adequately conceive them in one
of their elements, their infinity. But we can conceive them in their
other elements, which are the very same in the infinite as in the finite
development. Anything carried to the infinite must have all the properties of the same thing as finite, except those which depend upon the
finiteness. Among the many who have said that we cannot conceive
infinite space, did anyone ever suppose that it is *not* space? that it does
not possess all the properties by which space is characterized? Infinite
space cannot be cubical or spherical, because these are modes of being
bounded: but does anyone imagine that in ranging through it we might
arrive at some region which was not extended; of which one part was
not outside another; where, though no Body intervened, motion was
impossible; or where the sum of two sides of a triangle was less than
the third side? The parallel assertion may be made respecting infinite
goodness. What belongs to it as Infinite (or more properly as Absolute)
I do not pretend to know; but I know that infinite goodness must be
goodness, and that what is not consistent with goodness, is not consistent with infinite goodness. If in ascribing goodness to God I do
not mean what I mean by goodness; if I do not mean the goodness of
which I have some knowledge, but an incomprehensible attribute of
an incomprehensible substance, which for aught I know may be a totally
different quality from that which I love and venerate—and even must,
if Mr. Mansel is to be believed, be in some important particulars
opposed to this—what do I mean by calling it goodness? and what
reason have I for venerating it? If I know nothing about what the
attribute is, I cannot tell that it is a proper object of veneration. To
say that God's goodness may be different in kind from man's goodness,
what is it but saying, with a slight change of phraseology, that God

may possibly not be good? To assert in words what we do not think in meaning, is as suitable a definition as can be given of a moral falsehood. Besides, suppose that certain unknown attributes are ascribed to the Deity in a religion the external evidences of which are so conclusive to my mind, as effectually to convince me that it comes from God. Unless I believe God to possess the same moral attributes which I find, in however inferior a degree, in a good man, what ground of assurance have I of God's veracity? All trust in a Revelation presupposes a conviction that God's attributes are the same, in all but degree, with the best human attributes.

If, instead of the "glad tidings" that there exists a Being in whom all the excellences which the highest human mind can conceive, exist in a degree inconceivable to us, I am informed that the world is ruled by a being whose attributes are infinite, but what they are we cannot learn, nor what are the principles of his government, except that "the highest human morality which we are capable of conceiving" does not sanction them; convince me of it, and I will bear my fate as I may. But when I am told that I must believe this, and at the same time call this being by the names which express and affirm the highest human morality, I say in plain terms that I will not. Whatever power such a being may have over me, there is one thing which he shall not do: he shall not compel me to worship him. I will call no being good, who is not what I mean when I apply that epithet to my fellow-creatures; and if such a being can sentence me to hell for not so calling him, to hell I will go.

Neither is this to set up my own limited intellect as a criterion of divine or of any other wisdom. If a person is wiser and better than myself, not in some unknown and unknowable meaning of the terms, but in their known human acceptation, I am ready to believe that what this person thinks may be true, and that what he does may be right, when, but for the opinion I have of him, I should think otherwise. But this is because I believe that he and I have at bottom the same standard of truth and rule of right, and that he probably understands better than I the facts of the particular case. If I thought it not improbable that his notion of right might be my notion of wrong, I should not defer to his judgment. In like manner, one who sincerely believes in an absolutely good ruler of the world, is not warranted in disbelieving

any act ascribed to him, merely because the very small part of its
circumstances which we can possibly know does not sufficiently justify
it. But if what I am told respecting him is of a kind which no facts
that can be supposed added to my knowledge could make me perceive
to be right; if his alleged ways of dealing with the world are such
as no imaginable hypothesis respecting things known to him and unknown to me, could make consistent with the goodness and wisdom
which I mean when I use the terms, but are in direct contradiction to
their signification; then, if the law of contradiction is a law of human
thoughts, I cannot both believe these things and believe that God is
a good and wise being. If I call any being wise or good, not meaning
the only qualities which the words import, I am speaking insincerely;
I am flattering him by epithets which I fancy that he likes to hear,
in the hope of winning him over to my own objects. For it is worthy
of remark that the doubt whether words applied to God have their
human signification, is only felt when the words relate to his moral
attributes; it is never heard of in regard to his power. We are never
told that God's omnipotence must not be supposed to mean an infinite
degree of the power we know in man and nature, and that perhaps
it does not mean that he is able to kill us, or consign us to eternal
flames. The Divine Power is always interpreted in a completely human
signification, but the Divine Goodness and Justice must be understood
to be such only in an unintelligible sense. Is it unfair to surmise that
this is because those who speak in the name of God, have need of the
human conception of his power, since an idea which can overawe and
enforce obedience, must address itself to real feelings; but are content
that his goodness should be conceived only as something inconceivable,
because they are not often required to teach doctrines respecting him
which conflict irreconcilably with all goodness that we can conceive?

I am anxious to say once more, that Mr. Mansel's conclusions do not
go the whole length of his arguments, and that he disavows the doctrine
that God's justice and goodness are *wholly* different from what human
beings understand by the terms. He would, and does, admit that the
qualities as conceived by us bear *some likeness* to the justice and goodness which belong to God, since man was made in God's image. But
such a semi-concession, which no Christian could avoid making, since
without it the whole Christian scheme would be subverted, cannot

save him; he is not relieved by it from any difficulties, while it destroys the whole fabric of his argument. The Divine goodness, which is said to be a different thing from human goodness, but of which the human conception of goodness is some imperfect reflection or resemblance, does it agree with what men call goodness in the *essence* of the quality— in what *constitutes* it goodness? If it does, the "Rationalists" are right; it is not illicit to reason from the one to the other. If not, the divine attribute, whatever else it may be, is not goodness, and ought not to be called by the name. Unless there is some human conception which agrees with it, no human name can properly be applied to it; it is simply the unknown attribute of a thing unknown; it has no existence in relation to us, we can affirm nothing of it, and owe it no worship. Such is the inevitable alternative.

To conclude: . . . The proposition, that we cannot conceive the moral attributes of God in such a manner as to be able to affirm of any doctrine or assertion that it is inconsistent with them, has no foundation in the laws of the human mind: while if admitted, it would not prove that we should ascribe to God attributes bearing the same name as human qualities, but not to be understood in the same sense: it would prove that we ought not to ascribe any moral attributes to God at all, inasmuch as no moral attributes known or conceivable by us are true of him, and we are condemned to absolute ignorance of him as a moral being.

EVIL AND OMNIPOTENCE

J. L. MACKIE

The traditional arguments for the existence of God have been fairly thoroughly criticized by philosophers. But the theologian can, if he wishes, accept this criticism. He can admit that no rational proof of God's existence is possible. And he can still retain all that is essential to his position, by holding that God's existence is known in some other, nonrational way. I think, however, that a more telling criticism can be made by way of the traditional problem of evil. Here it can be shown, not that religious beliefs lack rational support, but that they are positively irrational, that the several parts of the essential theological doctrine are inconsistent with one another, so that the theologian can maintain his position as a whole only by a much more extreme rejection of reason than in the former case. He must now be prepared to believe,

From Mind, *Vol. LXIV, No. 254 (1955). Reprinted by permission of the author and the editor of* Mind.

not merely what cannot be proved, but what can be *disproved* from other beliefs that he also holds.

The problem of evil, in the sense in which I shall be using the phrase, is a problem only for someone who believes that there is a God who is both omnipotent and wholly good. And it is a logical problem, the problem of clarifying and reconciling a number of beliefs: it is not a scientific problem that might be solved by further observations, or a practical problem that might be solved by a decision or an action. These points are obvious; I mention them only because they are sometimes ignored by theologians, who sometimes parry a statement of the problem with such remarks as "Well, can you solve the problem yourself?" or "This is a mystery which may be revealed to us later" or "Evil is something to be faced and overcome, not to be merely discussed."

In its simplest form the problem is this: God is omnipotent; God is wholly good; and yet evil exists. There seems to be some contradiction between these three propositions, so that if any two of them were true the third would be false. But at the same time all three are essential parts of most theological positions: the theologian, it seems, at once *must* adhere and *cannot consistently* adhere to all three. (The problem does not arise only for theists, but I shall discuss it in the form in which it presents itself for ordinary theism.)

However, the contradiction does not arise immediately; to show it we need some additional premises, or perhaps some quasi-logical rules connecting the terms "good," "evil," and "omnipotent." These additional principles are that good is opposed to evil, in such a way that a good thing always eliminates evil as far as it can, and that there are no limits to what an omnipotent thing can do. From these it follows that a good omnipotent thing eliminates evil completely, and then the propositions that a good omnipotent thing exists, and that evil exists, are incompatible.

ADEQUATE SOLUTIONS

Now once the problem is fully stated it is clear that it can be solved, in the sense that the problem will not arise if one gives up at least one of the propositions that constitute it. If you are prepared to say that God is not wholly good, or not quite omnipotent, or that evil does not exist, or that good is not opposed to the kind of evil that exists, or that there are limits to what an omnipotent thing can do, then the problem of evil will not arise for you.

There are, then, quite a number of adequate solutions of the problem of evil, and some of these have been adopted, or almost adopted, by various thinkers. For example, a few have been prepared to deny God's omnipotence, and rather more have been prepared to keep the term "omnipotence" but severely to restrict its meaning, recording quite a number of things that an omnipotent being cannot do. Some have said that evil is an illusion, perhaps because they held that the whole world of temporal, changing things is an illusion, and that what we call evil belongs only to this world, or perhaps because they held that although temporal things *are* much as we see them, those that we call evil are not really evil. Some have said that what we call evil is merely the privation of good, that evil in a positive sense, evil that would really be opposed to good, does not exist. Many have agreed with Pope that disorder is harmony not understood, and that partial evil is universal good. Whether any of these views is *true* is, of course, another question. But each of them gives an adequate solution of the problems of evil in the sense that if you accept it this problem does not arise for you, though you may, of course, have *other* problems to face.

But often enough these adequate solutions are only *almost* adopted. The thinkers who restrict God's power, but keep the term "omnipotence," may reasonably be suspected of thinking, in other contexts, that his power is really unlimited. Those who say that evil is an illusion may also be thinking, inconsistently, that this illusion is itself an evil. Those who say that "evil" is merely privation of good may also be thinking, inconsistently, that privation of good is an evil. (The fallacy here is akin to some forms of the "naturalistic fallacy" in ethics, where some think, for example, that "good" is just what contributes to evolutionary progress, and that evolutionary progress is itself good.) If Pope meant what he said in the first line of his couplet, that "disorder" is only harmony not understood, the "partial evil" of the second line must, for consistency, mean "that which, taken in isolation, falsely appears to be evil," but it would more naturally mean "that which, in isolation, really is evil." The second line, in fact, hesitates between two views, that "partial evil" isn't really evil, since only the universal quality is real, and that "partial evil" is really an evil, but only a little one.

In addition, therefore, to adequate solutions, we must recognize unsatisfactory inconsistent solutions, in which there is only a half-hearted or temporary rejection of one of the propositions which together constitute the problem. In these, one of the constituent propositions is explicitly rejected, but it is covertly reasserted or assumed elsewhere in the system.

FALLACIOUS SOLUTIONS

Besides these half-hearted solutions, which explicitly reject but implicitly assert one of the constituent propositions, there are definitely fallacious solutions which explicitly maintain all the constituent propositions, but implicitly reject at least one of them in the course of the argument that explains away the problem of evil.

There are, in fact, many so-called solutions which purport to remove the contradiction without abandoning any of its constituent propositions. These must be fallacious, as we can see from the very statement of the problem, but it is not so easy to see in each case precisely where the fallacy lies. I suggest that in all cases the fallacy has the general form suggested above: in order to solve the problem one (or perhaps more) of its constituent propositions is given up, but in such a way that it appears to have been retained, and can therefore be asserted without qualification in other contexts. Sometimes there is a further complication: the supposed solution moves to and fro between, say, two of the constituent propositions, at one point asserting the first of these but covertly abandoning the second, at another point asserting the second but covertly abandoning the first. These fallacious solutions often turn upon some equivocation with the words "good" and "evil," or upon some vagueness about the way in which good and evil are opposed to one another, or about how much is meant by "omnipotence." I propose to examine some of these so-called solutions, and to exhibit their fallacies in detail. Incidentally, I shall also be considering whether an adequate solution could be reached by a minor modification of one or more of the constituent propositions, which would, however, still satisfy all the essential requirements of ordinary theism.

1. "Good cannot exist without evil" or "Evil is necessary as a counterpart to good."

It is sometimes suggested that evil is necessary as a counterpart to good, that if there were no evil there could be no good either, and that this solves the problem of evil. It is true that it points to an answer to the question "Why should there be evil?" But it does so only by qualifying some of the propositions that constitute the problem.

First, it sets a limit to what God can do, saying that God *cannot* create good without simultaneously creating evil, and this means either that God is not omnipotent or that there are *some* limits to what an omnipotent thing can do. It may be replied that these limits are always presupposed, that omnipotence has never meant the power to do what is logically impossible, and on the present view the existence of good without evil would be a logical impossibility. This interpretation of omnipotence may, indeed, be accepted as a modification of our original account which does not reject anything that is essential to theism, and I shall in general assume it in the subsequent discussion. It is, perhaps, the most common theistic view, but I think that some theists at least have maintained that God can do what is logically impossible. Many theists, at any rate, have held that logic itself is created or laid down by God, that logic is the way in which God arbitrarily chooses to think. (This is, of course, parallel to the ethical view that morally right actions are those which God arbitrarily chooses to command, and the two views encounter similar difficulties.) And *this* account of logic is clearly inconsistent with the view that God is bound by logical necessities—unless it is possible for an omnipotent being to bind himself, an issue which we shall consider later, when we come to the Paradox of Omnipotence. This solution of the problem of evil cannot, therefore, be consistently adopted along with the view that logic is itself created by God.

But, secondly, this solution denies that evil is opposed to good in our original sense. If good and evil are counterparts, a good thing will not "eliminate evil as far as it can." Indeed, this view suggests that good and evil are not strictly qualities of things at all. Perhaps the suggestion is that good and evil are related in much the same way as great and small. Certainly, when the term "great" is used relatively as a

condensation of "greater than so-and-so," and "small" is used correspondingly, greatness and smallness are counterparts and cannot exist
without each other. But in this sense greatness is not a quality, not
an intrinsic feature of anything; and it would be absurd to think of
a movement in favor of greatness and against smallness in this sense.
Such a movement would be self-defeating, since relative greatness can
be promoted only by a simultaneous promotion of relative smallness.
I feel sure that no theists would be content to regard God's goodness
as analogous to this—as if what he supports were not the *good* but the
better, and as if he had the paradoxical aim that all things should be
better than other things.

This point is obscured by the fact that "great" and "small" seem to
have an absolute as well as a relative sense. I cannot discuss here
whether there is absolute magnitude or not, but if there is, there could
be an absolute sense for "great," it could mean of at least a certain
size, and it would make sense to speak of all things getting bigger, of
a universe that was expanding all over, and therefore it would make
sense to speak of promoting greatness. But in *this* sense great and small
are not logically necessary counterparts: either quality could exist without the other. There would be no logical impossibility in everything's
being small or in everything's being great.

Neither in the absolute nor in the relative sense, then, of "great"
and "small" do these terms provide an analogy of the sort that would
be needed to support this solution of the problem of evil. In neither
case are greatness and smallness *both* necessary counterparts *and* mutually opposed forces or possible objects for support and attack.

It may be replied that good and evil are necessary counterparts in
the same way as any quality and its logical opposite: redness can occur,
it is suggested, only if nonredness also occurs. But unless evil is merely
the privation of good, they are not logical opposites, and some further
argument would be needed to show that they are counterparts in the
same way as genuine logical opposites. Let us assume that this could
be given. There is still doubt of the correctness of the metaphysical
principle that a quality must have a real opposite: I suggest that it is
not really impossible that everything should be, say, red, that the truth
is merely that if everything were red we should not notice redness,
and so we should have no word "red"; we observe and give names to

qualities only if they have real opposites. If so, the principle that a term must have an opposite would belong only to our language or to our thought, and would not be an ontological principle, and, correspondingly, the rule that good cannot exist without evil would not state a logical necessity of a sort that God would just have to put up with. God might have made everything good, though *we* should not have noticed it if he had.

But, finally, even if we concede that this *is* an ontological principle, it will provide a solution for the problem of evil only if one is prepared to say, "Evil exists, but only just enough evil to serve as the counterpart of good." I doubt whether any theist will accept this. After all, the *ontological* requirement that nonredness should occur would be satisfied even if all the universe, except for a minute speck, were red, and, if there were a corresponding requirement for evil as a counterpart to good, a minute dose of evil would presumably do. But theists are not usually willing to say, in all contexts, that all the evil that occurs is a minute and necessary dose.

2. "Evil is necessary as a means to good."

It is sometimes suggested that evil is necessary for good not as a counterpart but as a means. In its simple form this has little plausibility as a solution of the problem of evil, since it obviously implies a severe restriction of God's power. It would be a *causal* law that you cannot have a certain end without a certain means, so that if God has to introduce evil as a means to good, he must be subject to at least some causal laws. This certainly conflicts with what a theist normally means by omnipotence. This view of God as limited by causal laws also conflicts with the view that causal laws are themselves made by God, which is more widely held than the corresponding view about the laws of logic. This conflict would, indeed, be resolved if it were possible for an omnipotent being to bind himself, and this possibility has still to be considered. Unless a favorable answer can be given to this question, the suggestion that evil is necessary as a means to good solves the problem of evil only by denying one of its constituent propositions, either that God is omnipotent or that "omnipotent" means what it says.

3. "The universe is better with some evil in it than it could be if there were no evil."

Much more important is a solution which at first seems to be a mere variant of the previous one, that evil may contribute to the goodness of a whole in which it is found, so that the universe as a whole is better as it is, with some evil in it, than it would be if there were no evil. This solution may be developed in either of two ways. It may be supported by an aesthetic analogy, by the fact that contrasts heighten beauty, that in a musical work, for example, there may occur discords which somehow add to the beauty of the work as a whole. Alternatively, it may be worked out in connection with the notion of progress, that the best possible organization of the universe will not be static, but progressive, that the gradual overcoming of evil by good is really a finer thing than would be the eternal unchallenged supremacy of good

In either case, this solution usually starts from the assumption that the evil whose existence gives rise to the problem of evil is primarily what is called physical evil, that is to say, pain. In Hume's rather half-hearted presentation of the problem of evil, the evils that he stresses are pain and disease, and those who reply to him argue that the existence of pain and disease makes possible the existence of sympathy, benevolence, heroism, and the gradually successful struggle of doctors and reformers to overcome these evils. In fact, theists often seize the opportunity to accuse those who stress the problem of evil of taking a low, materialistic view of good and evil, equating these with pleasure and pain, and of ignoring the more spiritual goods which can arise in the struggle against evils.

But let us see exactly what is being done here. Let us call pain and misery "first order evil" or "evil (1)." What contrasts with this, namely, pleasure and happiness, will be called "first order good" or "good (1)." Distinct from this is "second order good" or "good (2)" which somehow emerges in a complex situation in which evil (1) is a necessary component—logically, not merely causally, necessary. (Exactly *how* it emerges does not matter: in the crudest version of this solution good [2] is simply the heightening of happiness by the contrast with misery, in other versions it includes sympathy with suffering, heroism in facing danger, and the gradual decrease of first order evil and increase of first order good.) It is also being assumed that second order good is more important than first order good or evil, in particular that it more than outweighs the first order evil it involves.

Now this is a particularly subtle attempt to solve the problem of evil. It defends God's goodness and omnipotence on the ground that (on a sufficiently long view) this is the best of all logically possible worlds, because it includes the important second order goods, and yet it admits that real evils, namely first order evils, exist. But does it still hold that good and evil are opposed? Not, clearly, in the sense that we set out originally: good does not tend to eliminate evil in general. Instead, we have a modified, a more complex pattern. First order good (e.g., happiness) *contrasts with* first order evil (e.g., misery) : these two are opposed in a fairly mechanical way; some second order goods (e.g., benevolence) try to maximize first order good and minimize first order evil; but God's goodness is not this, it is rather the will to maximize *second* order good. We might, therefore, call God's goodness an example of a third order goodness, or good (3). While this account is different from our original one, it might well be held to be an improvement on it, to give a more accurate description of the way in which good is opposed to evil, and to be consistent with the essential theist position.

There might, however, be several objections to this solution.

First, some might argue that such qualities as benevolence—and a fortiori the third order goodness which promotes benevolence—have a merely derivative value, that they are not higher sorts of good, but merely means to good (1), that is, to happiness, so that it would be absurd for God to keep misery in existence in order to make possible the virtues of benevolence, heroism, etc. The theist who adopts the present solution must, of course, deny this, but he can do so with some plausibility, so I should not press this objection.

Secondly, it follows from this solution that God is not in our sense benevolent or sympathetic: he is not concerned to minimize evil (1), but only to promote good (2) ; and this might be a disturbing conclusion for some theists.

But, thirdly, the fatal objection is this. Our analysis shows clearly the possibility of the existence of a *second* order evil, an evil (2) contrasting with good (2) as evil (1) contrasts with good (1). This would include malevolence, cruelty, callousness, cowardice, and states in which good

(1) is decreasing and evil (1) increasing. And just as good (2) is held to be the important kind of good, the kind that God is concerned to promote, so evil (2) will, by analogy, be the important kind of evil, the kind which God, if he were wholly good and omnipotent, would eliminate. And yet evil (2) plainly exists, and indeed most theists (in other contexts) stress its existence more than that of evil (1). We should, therefore, state the problem of evil in terms of second order evil, and against this form of the problem the present solution is useless.

An attempt might be made to use this solution again, at a higher level, to explain the occurrence of evil (2): indeed the next main solution that we shall examine does just this, with the help of some new notions. Without any fresh notions, such a solution would have little plausibility: for example, we could hardly say that the really important good was a good (3), such as the increase of benevolence in proportion to cruelty, which logically required for its occurrence the occurrence of some second order evil. But even if evil (2) could be explained in this way, it is fairly clear that there would be third order evils contrasting with this third order good: and we should be well on the way to an infinite regress, where the solution of a problem of evil, stated in terms of evil (n), indicated the existence of an evil $(n + 1)$, and a further problem to be solved.

4. "Evil is due to human free will."

Perhaps the most important proposed solution of the problem of evil is that evil is not to be ascribed to God at all, but to the independent actions of human beings, supposed to have been endowed by God with freedom of the will. This solution may be combined with the preceding one: first order evil (e.g., pain) may be justified as a logically necessary component in second order good (e.g., sympathy) while second order evil (e.g., cruelty) is not *justified,* but is so ascribed to human beings that God cannot be held responsible for it. This combination evades my third criticism of the preceding solution.

The free-will solution also involves the preceding solution at a higher level. To explain why a wholly good God gave men free will although it would lead to some important evils, it must be argued that it is better on the whole that men should act freely, and sometimes err, than that they should be innocent automata, acting rightly in a wholly determined way. Freedom, that is to say, is now treated as a third order good, and as being more valuable than second order goods (such as sympathy and heroism) would be if they were deterministically produced, and it is being assumed that second order evils, such as cruelty, are logically necessary accompaniments of freedom, just as pain is a logically necessary precondition of sympathy.

I think that this solution is unsatisfactory primarily because of the incoherence of the notion of freedom of the will: but I cannot discuss this topic adequately here, although some of my criticisms will touch upon it.

First I should query the assumption that second order evils are logically necessary accompaniments of freedom. I should ask this: if God has made men such that in their free choices they sometimes prefer what is good and sometimes what is evil, why could he not have made men such that they always freely choose the good? If there is no logical impossibility in a man's freely choosing the good on one, or on several, occasions, there cannot be a logical impossibility in his freely choosing the good on every occasion. God was not, then, faced with a choice between making innocent automata and making beings who, in acting freely, would sometimes go wrong: there was open to him the obviously better possibility of making beings who would act freely but always go right. Clearly, his failure to avail himself of this possibility is inconsistent with his being both omnipotent and wholly good.

If it is replied that this objection is absurd, that the making of some wrong choices is logically necessary for freedom, it would seem that "freedom" must here mean complete randomness or indeterminacy, including randomness with regard to the alternatives good and evil, in other words that men's choices and consequent actions can be "free" only if they are not determined by their characters. Only on this assumption can God escape the responsibility for men's actions; for if he made them as they are, but did not determine their wrong choices, this can only be because the wrong choices are not determined by men as they are. But then if freedom is randomness, how can it be a characteristic of *will*? And, still more, how can it be the most important good? What value or merit would there be in free choices if these were random actions which were not determined by the nature of the agent?

I conclude that to make this solution plausible two different senses of "freedom" must be confused, one sense which will justify the view that freedom is a third order good, more valuable than other goods would be without it, and another sense, sheer randomness, to prevent us from ascribing to God a decision to make men such that they sometimes go wrong when he might have made them such that they would always freely go right.

This criticism is sufficient to dispose of this solution. But besides this there is a fundamental difficulty in the notion of an omnipotent God creating men with free will, for if men's wills are really free this must mean that even God cannot control them, that is, that God is no longer omnipotent. It may be objected that God's gift of freedom to men does not mean that he *cannot* control their wills, but that he always *refrains* from controlling their wills. But why, we may ask, should God refrain from controlling evil wills? Why should he not leave men free to will rightly, but intervene when he sees them beginning to will wrongly? If God could do this, but does not, and if he is wholly good, the only explanation could be that even a wrong free act of will is not really evil, that its freedom is a value which outweighs its wrongness, so that there would be a loss of value if God took away the wrongness and the freedom together. But this is utterly opposed to what theists say about sin in other contexts. The present solution of the problem of evil, then, can be maintained only in the form that God has made men so free that he *cannot* control their wills.

This leads us to what I call the "Paradox of Omnipotence": can an omnipotent being make things which he cannot subsequently control? Or, what is practically equivalent to this, can an omnipotent being make rules which then bind himself? (These are practically equivalent because any such rules could be regarded as setting certain things beyond his control, and vice versa.) The second of these formulations is relevant to the suggestions that we have already met, that an omnipotent God creates the rules of logic or causal laws, and is then bound by them.

It is clear that this is a paradox: the questions cannot be answered satisfactorily either in the affirmative or in the negative. If we answer "Yes," it follows that if God actually makes things which he cannot control, or makes rules which bind himself, he is not omnipotent once he had made them: there are *then* things which he cannot do. But if we answer "No," we are immediately asserting that there are things which he cannot do, that is to say that he is already not omnipotent.

It cannot be replied that the question which sets this paradox is not a proper question. It would make perfectly good sense to say that a human mechanic has made a machine which he cannot control: if there is any difficulty about the question it lies in the notion of omnipotence itself.

This, incidentally, shows that although we have approached this paradox from the free-will theory, it is equally a problem for a theological determinist. No one thinks that machines have free will, yet they may well be beyond the control of their makers. The determinist might reply that anyone who makes anything determines its ways of acting, and so determines its subsequent behavior: even the human mechanic does this by his *choice* of materials and structure for his machine, though he does not know all about either of these: the mechanic thus determines, though he may not foresee, his machine's actions. And since God is omniscient, and since his creation of things is total, he both determines and foresees the ways in which his creatures will act. We may grant this, but it is beside the point. The question is not whether God *originally* determined the future actions of his creatures, but whether he can *subsequently* control their actions, or whether he was able in his original creation to put things beyond his subsequent control. Even on determinist principles the answers "Yes" and "No" are equally irreconcilable with God's omnipotence.

Before suggesting a solution of this paradox, I would point out that there is a parallel Paradox of Sovereignty. Can a legal sovereign make a law restricting its own future legislative power? For example, could the British parliament make a law forbidding any future parliament to socialize banking, and also forbidding the future repeal of this law itself? Or could the British parliament, which was legally sovereign in Australia in, say, 1899, pass a valid law, or series of laws, which made it no longer sovereign in 1933? Again, neither the affirmative nor the negative answer is really satisfactory. If we were to answer "Yes," we should be admitting the validity of a law which, if it were actually made, would mean that parliament was no longer sovereign. If we were to answer "No," we should be admitting that there is a law, not logically absurd, which parliament cannot validly make, that is, that parliament is not now a legal sovereign. This paradox can be solved in the following way. We should distinguish between first order laws, that is laws governing the actions of individuals and bodies other than the legislature, and second order laws, that is laws about laws, laws governing the actions of the legislature itself. Correspondingly, we should distinguish two orders of sovereignty, first order sovereignty (sovereignty [1]) which is unlimited authority to make first order laws, and second order sovereignty (sovereignty [2]) which is unlimited authority to make second order laws. If we say that parliament is sovereign we might mean that any parliament at any time has sovereignty (1), or we might mean that parliament has both sovereignty (1) and sovereignty (2) at present, but we cannot without contradiction mean both that the present parliament has sovereignty (2) and that every parliament at every time has sovereignty (1), for if the present parliament has sovereignty (2) it may use it to take away the sovereignty (1) of later parliaments. What the paradox shows is that we cannot ascribe to any continuing institution legal sovereignty in an inclusive sense.

The analogy between omnipotence and sovereignty shows that the paradox of omnipotence can be solved in a similar way. We must distinguish between first order omnipotence (omnipotence [1]), that is unlimited power to act, and second order omnipotence (omnipotence [2]), that is unlimited power to determine what powers to act things shall have. Then we could consistently say that God all the time has omnipotence (1), but if so no beings at any time have powers to act independently of God. Or we could say that God at one time had omnipotence (2), and used it to assign independent powers to act to certain things, so that God thereafter did not have omnipotence (1). But what the paradox shows is that we cannot consistently ascribe to any continuing being omnipotence in an inclusive sense.

An alternative solution of this paradox would be simply to deny that God is a continuing being, that any times can be assigned to his actions at all. But on this assumption (which also has difficulties of its own) no meaning can be given to the assertion that God made men with wills so free that he could not control them. The paradox of omnipotence can be avoided by putting God outside time, but the free-will solution of the problem of evil cannot be saved in this way, and equally it remains impossible to hold that an omnipotent God *binds himself* by causal or logical laws.

CONCLUSION

Of the proposed solutions of the problem of evil which we have examined, none has stood up to criticism. There may be other solutions
which require examination, but this study strongly suggests that there
is no valid solution of the problem which does not modify at least one of
the constituent propositions in a way which would seriously affect the
essential core of the theistic position.

Quite apart from the problem of evil, the paradox of omnipotence has
shown that God's omnipotence must in any case be restricted in one way
or another, that unqualified omnipotence cannot be ascribed to any being
that continues through time. And if God and his actions are not in time,
can omnipotence, or power of any sort, be meaningfully ascribed to him?

GOD AND EVIL

H. J. McCLOSKEY

THE PROBLEM STATED

Evil is a problem for the theist in that a contradiction is involved in the fact of evil on the one hand, and the belief in the omnipotence and perfection of God on the other. God cannot be both all-powerful and perfectly good if evil is real. This contradiction is well set out in its detail by Mackie in his discussion of the problem.[1] In his discussion Mackie seeks to show that this contradiction cannot be resolved in terms of man's free will. In arguing in this way Mackie neglects a large number of important points, and concedes far too much to the theist. He implicitly allows that while physical evil creates a problem, this problem

From The Philosophical Quarterly, *Vol. X, No. 39 (1960). Reprinted by per mission of the author and the editors of* The Philosophical Quarterly.

[1] "Evil and Omnipotence." (See above, pp. 46ff.)

is reducible to the problem of moral evil and that therefore the satisfactoriness of solutions of the problem of evil turns on the compatibility of free will and absolute goodness. In fact physical evils create a number of distinct problems which are not reducible to the problem of moral evil. Further, the proposed solution of the problem of moral evil in terms of free will renders the attempt to account for physical evil in terms of moral good, and the attempt thereby to reduce the problem of evil to the problem of moral evil, completely untenable. Moreover, the account of moral evil in terms of free will breaks down on more obvious and less disputable grounds than those indicated by Mackie. Moral evil can be shown to remain a problem whether or not free will is compatible with absolute goodness. I therefore propose in this paper to reopen the discussion of "the problem of evil," by approaching it from a more general standpoint, examining a wider variety of solutions than those considered by Mackie and his critics.

The fact of evil creates a problem for the theist; but there are a number of simple solutions available to a theist who is content seriously to modify his theism. He can either admit a limit to God's power, or he can deny God's moral perfection. He can assert either (1) that God is not powerful enough to make a world that does not contain evil, or (2) that God created only the good in the universe and that some other power created the evil, or (3) that God is all-powerful but morally imperfect, and chose to create an imperfect universe. Few Christians accept these solutions, and this is no doubt partly because such "solutions" ignore the real inspiration of religious beliefs, and partly because they introduce embarrassing complications for the theist in his attempts to deal with other serious problems. However, if any one of these "solutions" is accepted, then the problem of evil is avoided, and a weakened version of theism is made secure from attacks based upon the fact of the occurrence of evil.

For more orthodox theism, according to which God is both omnipotent and perfectly good, evil creates a real problem; and this problem is well stated by the Jesuit, Father G. H. Joyce. Joyce writes:

> The existence of evil in the world must at all times be the greatest of all problems which the mind encounters when it reflects on God and His relation to the world. If He is, indeed, all-good and all-powerful, how has evil any place in the world which He has made? Whence came it? Why is it here? If He is all-good why did

He allow it to arise? If all-powerful why does He not deliver us from the burden? Alike in the physical and moral order creation seems so grievously marred that we find it hard to understand how it can derive in its entirety from God.[2]

The facts which give rise to the problem are of two general kinds, and give rise to two distinct types of problem. These two general kinds of evil are usually referred to as "physical" and as "moral" evil. These terms are by no means apt—suffering for instance is not strictly physical evil—and they conceal significant differences. However, this terminology is too widely accepted, and too convenient to be dispensed with here, the more especially as the various kinds of evil, while important as distinct kinds, need not for our purposes be designated by separate names.

Physical evil and moral evil then are the two general forms of evil which independently and jointly constitute conclusive grounds for denying the existence of God in the sense defined, namely as an all-powerful, perfect Being. The acuteness of these two general problems is evident when we consider the nature and extent of the evils of which account must be given. To take physical evils, looking first at the less important of these.

(a) *Physical evils:* Physical evils are involved in the very constitution of the earth and animal kingdom. There are deserts and icebound areas; there are dangerous animals of prey, as well as creatures such as scorpions and snakes. There are also pests such as flies and fleas and the hosts of other insect pests, as well as the multitude of lower parasites such as tapeworms, hookworms and the like. Secondly, there are the various natural calamities and the immense human suffering that follows in their wake —fires, floods, tempests, tidal waves, volcanoes, earthquakes, droughts and famines. Thirdly, there are the vast numbers of diseases that torment and ravage man. Diseases such as leprosy, cancer, poliomyelitis, appear *prima facie* not to be creations which are to be expected of a benevolent Creator. Fourthly, there are the evils with which so many are born— the various physical deformities and defects such as misshapen limbs, blindness, deafness, dumbness, mental deficiency and insanity. Most of these evils contribute towards increasing human pain and suffering; but not all physical evils are reducible simply to pain. Many of these evils are evils whether or not they result in pain. This is important, for it means

---

[2] Joyce, *Principles of Natural Theology,* Chap. 17. All subsequent quotations from Joyce in this paper are from this chapter of this work.

that, unless there is one solution to such diverse evils, it is both inaccurate and positively misleading to speak of *the* problem of physical evil. Shortly I shall be arguing that no one "solution" covers all these evils, so we shall have to conclude that physical evils create not one problem but a number of distinct problems for the theist.

The nature of the various difficulties referred to by the theist as the problem of physical evil is indicated by Joyce in a way not untypical among the more honest, philosophical theists, as follows:

> The actual amount of suffering which the human race endures is immense. Disease has store and to spare of torments for the body: and disease and death are the lot to which we must all look forward. At all times, too, great numbers of the race are pinched by want. Nor is the world ever free for very long from the terrible sufferings which follow in the track of war. If we concentrate our attention on human woes, to the exclusion of the joys of life, we gain an appalling picture of the ills to which the flesh is heir. So too if we fasten our attention on the sterner side of nature, on the pains which men endure from natural forces—on the storms which wreck their ships, the cold which freezes them to death, the fire which consumes them —if we contemplate this aspect of nature alone we may be led to wonder how God came to deal so harshly with His Creatures as to provide them with such a home.

Many such statements of the problem proceed by suggesting, if not by stating, that the problem arises at least in part by concentrating one's attention too exclusively on one aspect of the world. This is quite contrary to the facts. The problem is not one that results from looking at only one aspect of the universe. It may be the case that over-all pleasure predominates over pain, and that physical goods in general predominate over physical evils, but the opposite may equally well be the case. It is both practically impossible and logically impossible for this question to be resolved. However, it is not an unreasonable presumption, with the large bulk of mankind inadequately fed and housed and without adequate medical and health services, to suppose that physical evils at present predominate over physical goods. In the light of the facts at our disposal, this would seem to be a much more reasonable conclusion than the conclusion hinted at by Joyce and openly advanced by less cautious theists, namely, that physical goods in fact outweigh physical evils in the world.

However, the question is not "Which predominates, physical good or physical evil?" The problem of physical evil remains a problem whether the balance in the universe is on the side of physical good or not, because the problem is that of accounting for the fact that physical evil occurs at all.

(b) *Moral evil:* Physical evils create one of the groups of problems referred to by the theist as "the problem of evil." Moral evil creates quite a distinct problem. Moral evil is simply immorality—evils such as selfishness, envy, greed, deceit, cruelty, callousness, cowardice and the larger scale evils such as wars and the atrocities they involve.

Moral evil is commonly regarded as constituting an even more serious problem than physical evil. Joyce so regards it, observing:

> The man who sins thereby offends God. . . . We are called on to explain how God came to create an order of things in which rebellion and even final rejection have such a place. Since a choice from among an infinite number of possible worlds lay open to God, how came He to choose one in which these occur? Is not such a choice in flagrant opposition to the Divine Goodness?

Some theists seek a solution by denying the reality of evil or by describing it as a "privation" or absence of good. They hope thereby to explain it away as not needing a solution. This, in the case of most of the evils which require explanation, seems to amount to little more than an attempt to sidestep the problem simply by changing the name of that which has to be explained. It can be exposed for what it is simply by describing some of the evils which have to be explained. That is why a survey of the data to be accounted for is a most important part of the discussion of the problem of evil.

In *The Brothers Karamazov,* Dostoevski introduces a discussion of the problem of evil by reference to some then recently committed atrocities. Ivan states the problem:

> "By the way, a Bulgarian I met lately in Moscow," Ivan went on . . . "told me about the crimes committed by Turks in all parts of Bulgaria through fear of a general rising of the Slavs. They burn villages, murder, outrage women and children, and nail their prisoners by the ears to the fences, leave them till morning, and in the morning hang them—all sorts of things you can't imagine. People talk sometimes of bestial cruelty, but that's a great injustice and insult to the beasts; a beast can never be so cruel as a man, so artistically cruel. The tiger only tears and gnaws and that's all he can do. He would never think of nailing people by the ears, even if he were able to do it. These Turks took a pleasure in torturing chil-

dren too; cutting the unborn child from the mother's womb, and tossing babies up in the air and catching them on the points of their bayonets before their mothers' eyes. Doing it before the mother's eyes was what gave zest to the amusement. Here is another scene that I thought very interesting. Imagine a trembling mother with her baby in her arms, a circle of invading Turks around her. They've planned a diversion: they pet the baby to make it laugh. They succeed; the baby laughs. At that moment, a Turk points a pistol four inches from the baby's face. The baby laughs with glee, holds out its little hands to the pistol, and he pulls the trigger in the baby's face and blows out its brains. Artistic, wasn't it?" [3]

Ivan's statement of the problem was based on historical events. Such happenings did not cease in the nineteenth century. *The Scourge of the Swastika* by Lord Russell of Liverpool contains little else than descriptions of such atrocities; and it is simply one of a host of writings giving documented lists of instances of evils, both physical and moral.

Thus the problem of evil is both real and acute. There is a clear *prima facie* case that evil and God are incompatible—both cannot exist. Most theists admit this, and that the onus is on them to show that the conflict is not fatal to theism; but a consequence is that a host of proposed solutions are advanced.

The mere fact of such a multiplicity of proposed solutions, and the widespread repudiation of each other's solutions by theists, in itself suggests that the fact of evil is an insuperable obstacle to theism as defined here. It also makes it impossible to treat of all proposed solutions, and all that can be attempted here is an examination of those proposed solutions which are most commonly invoked and most generally thought to be important by theists.

Some theists admit the reality of the problem of evil, and then seek to sidestep it, declaring it to be a great mystery which we poor humans cannot hope to comprehend. Other theists adopt a rational approach and advance rational arguments to show that evil, properly understood, is compatible with, and even a consequence of God's goodness. The arguments to be advanced in this paper are directed against the arguments of the latter theists; but in so far as these arguments are successful against the rational theists, to that extent they are also effective in show-

---

[3] Garnett translation (London: William Heinemann, Ltd., 1945).

ing that the nonrational approach in terms of great mysteries is positively irrational.

PROPOSED SOLUTIONS TO THE PROBLEM
OF PHYSICAL EVIL

Of the large variety of arguments advanced by theists as solutions to the problem of physical evil, five popularly used and philosophically significant solutions will be examined. They are, in brief: (1) Physical good (pleasure) requires physical evil (pain) to exist at all; (2) Physical evil is God's punishment of sinners; (3) Physical evil is God's warning and reminder to man; (4) Physical evil is the result of the natural laws, the operations of which are on the whole good; (5) Physical evil increases the total good.

1. *Physical Good Is Impossible without Physical Evil:* Pleasure is possible only by way of contrast with pain. Here the analogy of color is used. If everything were blue we should, it is argued, understand neither what color is nor what blue is. So with pleasure and pain.

The most obvious defect of such an argument is that it does not cover all physical goods and evils. It is an argument commonly invoked by those who think of physical evil as creating only one problem, namely the problem of human pain. However, the problems of physical evils are not reducible to the one problem, the problem of pain; hence the argument is simply irrelevant to much physical evil. Disease and insanity are evils, but health and sanity are possible in the total absence of disease and insanity. Further, if the argument were in any way valid even in respect of pain, it would imply the existence of only a speck of pain, and not the immense amount of pain in the universe. A speck of yellow is all that is needed for an appreciation of blueness and of color generally. The argument is therefore seen to be seriously defective on two counts even if its underlying principle is left unquestioned. If its underlying principle is questioned, the argument is seen to be essentially invalid. Can it seriously be maintained that if an individual were born crippled and deformed and never in his life experienced pleasure, that he could not experience pain, not even if he were severely injured? It is clear that pain is possible in the absence of pleasure. It is true that it might not be distinguished by a special name and called "pain," but the state we now describe as a painful state would nonetheless be possible in the total absence of pleasure. So too the converse would seem to apply. Plato brings this out very clearly in Book 9 of the *Republic* in respect of the pleasures of taste and smell. These pleasures seem not to depend for their existence on any prior experience of pain. Thus the argument is unsound in respect of its main contention; and in being unsound in this respect, it is at the same time ascribing a serious limitation to God's power. It maintains that God cannot create pleasure without creating pain, although as we have seen, pleasure and pain are not correlatives.

2. *Physical Evil Is God's Punishment for Sin:* This kind of explanation was advanced to explain the terrible Lisbon earthquake in the eighteenth century, in which 40,000 people were killed. There are many replies to this argument, for instance Voltaire's. Voltaire asked: "Did God in this earthquake select the 40,000 least virtuous of the Portuguese citizens?" The distribution of disease and pain is in no obvious way related to the virtue of the persons afflicted, and popular saying has it that the distribution is slanted in the opposite direction. The only way of meeting the fact that evils are not distributed proportionately to the evil of the sufferer is by suggesting that all human beings, including children, are such miserable sinners, that our offences are of such enormity, that God would be justified in punishing all of us as severely as it is possible for humans to be punished; but even then, God's apparent caprice in the selection of His victims requires explanation. In any case it is by no means clear that young children who very often suffer severely are guilty of sin of such an enormity as would be necessary to justify their sufferings as punishment.

Further, many physical evils are simultaneous with birth—insanity, mental defectiveness, blindness, deformities, as well as much disease. No crime or sin of *the child* can explain and justify these physical evils as punishment; and, for a parent's sin to be punished in the child is injustice or evil of another kind.

Similarly, the sufferings of animals cannot be accounted for as punishment. For these various reasons, therefore, this argument must be rejected. In fact it has dropped out of favor in philosophical and theological circles, but it continues to be invoked at the popular level.

3. *Physical Evil Is God's Warning to Men:* It is argued, for instance of physical calamities, that "they serve a moral end which compensates the physical evil which they cause. The awful nature of these phenomena, the overwhelming power of the forces at work, and man's utter helplessness before them, rouse him from the religious indifference to which he is so prone. They inspire a reverential awe of the Creator who made them, and controls them, and a salutary fear of violating the laws which He has imposed" (Joyce). This is where immortality is often alluded to as justifying evil.

This argument proceeds from a proposition that is plainly false; and that the proposition from which it proceeds is false is conceded implicitly by most theologians. Natural calamities do not necessarily turn people to God, but rather present the problem of evil in an acute form; and the problem of evil is said to account for more defections from religion than any other cause. Thus if God's object in bringing about natural calamities is to inspire reverence and awe, He is a bungler. There are many more reliable methods of achieving this end. Equally important, the use of physical evil to achieve this object is hardly the course one would expect a benevolent God to adopt when other, more effective, less evil methods are available to Him, for example, miracles, special revelation, etc.

4. *Evils Are the Results of the Operation of Laws of Nature:*[4] This fourth argument relates to most physical evil, but it is more usually used to account for animal suffering and physical calamities. These evils are said to result from the operation of the natural laws which govern these objects, the relevant natural laws being the various causal laws, the law of pleasure-pain as a law governing sentient beings, etc. The theist argues that the nonoccurrence of these evils would involve either the constant intervention by God in a miraculous way, and contrary to his own natural laws, or else the construction of a universe with different components subject to different laws of nature; for God, in creating a certain kind of being, must create it subject to its appropriate law; He cannot create it and subject it to any law of His own choosing. Hence He

---

[4] For further discussion of the proposed solutions treated in this and the following section see my article "The Problem of Evil," *Journal of Bible and Religion,* Vol. XXX, No. 3 (1962), esp. 188ff. [Note added to this edition.]

creates a world which has components and laws good in their total effect, although calamitous in some particular effects.

Against this argument three objections are to be urged. First, it does not cover all physical evil. Clearly not all disease can be accounted for along these lines. Secondly, it is not to give a reason against God's miraculous intervention simply to assert that it would be unreasonable for Him constantly to intervene in the operation of His own laws. Yet this is the only reason that theists seem to offer here. If, by intervening in respect to the operation of His laws, God could thereby eliminate an evil, it would seem to be unreasonable and evil of Him not to do so. Some theists seek a way out of this difficulty by denying that God has the power miraculously to intervene; but this is to ascribe a severe limitation to His power. It amounts to asserting that when His Creation has been effected, God can do nothing else except contemplate it. The third objection is related to this, and is to the effect that it is already to ascribe a serious limitation to God's omnipotence to suggest that He could not make sentient beings which did not experience pain, nor sentient beings without deformities and deficiencies, nor natural phenomena with different laws of nature governing them. There is no reason why better laws of nature governing the existing objects are not possible on the divine hypothesis. Surely, if God is all-powerful, He could have made a better universe in the first place, or one with better laws of nature governing it, so that the operation of its laws did not produce calamities and pain. To maintain this is not to suggest that an omnipotent God should be capable of achieving what is logically impossible. All that has been indicated here is logically possible, and therefore not beyond the powers of a being Who is really omnipotent.

This fourth argument seeks to exonerate God by explaining that He created a universe sound on the whole, but such that He had no direct control over the laws governing His creations, and had control only in His selection of His creations. The previous two arguments attribute the detailed results of the operations of these laws directly to God's will. Theists commonly use all three arguments. It is not without significance that they betray such uncertainty as to whether God is to be *commended* or *exonerated*.

5. *The Universe Is Better with Evil in It:* This is the important argument. One version of it runs:

Just as the human artist has in view the beauty of his composition as a whole, not making it his aim to give to each several part the highest degree of brilliancy, but that measure of adornment which most contributes to the combined effect, so it is with God (Joyce).

Another version of this general type of argument explains evil not so much as *a component* of a good whole, seen out of its context as a mere component, but rather as *a means* to a greater good. Different as these versions are, they may be treated here as one general type of argument, for the same criticisms are fatal to both versions.

This kind of argument if valid simply shows that some evil may enrich the Universe; it tells us nothing about *how much* evil will enrich this particular universe, and how much will be too much. So, even if valid in principle—and shortly I shall argue that it is not valid—such an argument does not in itself provide a justification for the evil in the universe. It shows simply that the evil which occurs might have a justification. In view of the immense amount of evil the probabilities are against it.

This is the main point made by Wisdom in his discussion of this argument. Wisdom sums up his criticism as follows:

It remains to add that, unless there are independent arguments in favor of this world's being the best logically possible world, it is probable that some of the evils in it are not logically necessary to a compensating good; it is probable because there are so many evils.[5]

Wisdom's reply brings out that the person who relies upon this argument as a conclusive and complete argument is seriously mistaken. The argument, if valid, justifies only some evil. A belief that it justifies all the evil that occurs in the world is mistaken, for a second argument, by way of a supplement to it, is needed. This supplementary argument would take the form of a proof that all the evil that occurs is *in fact* valuable and necessary as a means to greater good. Such a supplementary proof is in principle impossible; so, at best, this fifth argument can be taken to show only that some evil *may be* necessary for the production of good, and that the evil in the world may perhaps have a justification on this account. This is not to justify a physical evil, but simply to sug-

---

[5] *Mind*, Vol. XLIV, No. 173 (1931).

gest that physical evil might nonetheless have a justification, although we may never come to know this justification.

Thus the argument even if it is valid as a general form of reasoning is unsatisfactory because inconclusive. It is, however, also unsatisfactory in that it follows on the principle of the argument that, just as it is possible that evil in the total context contributes to increasing the total ultimate good, so equally, it will hold that good in the total context may increase the ultimate evil. Thus if the principle of the argument were sound, we could never know whether evil is really evil, or good really good. (Aesthetic analogies may be used to illustrate this point.) By implication it follows that it would be dangerous to eliminate evil because we may thereby introduce a discordant element into the divine symphony of the universe; and, conversely, it may be wrong to condemn the elimination of what is good, because the latter may result in the production of more, higher goods.

So it follows that, even if the general principle of the argument is not questioned, it is still seen to be a defective argument. On the one hand, it proves too little—it justifies only some evil and not necessarily all the evil in the universe; on the other hand it proves too much because it creates doubts about the goodness of apparent goods. These criticisms in themselves are fatal to the argument as a solution to the problem of physical evil. However, because this is one of the most popular and plausible accounts of physical evil, it is worthwhile considering whether it can properly be claimed to establish even the very weak conclusion indicated above.

Why, and in what way, is it supposed that physical evils such as pain and misery, disease and deformity, will heighten the total effect and add to the value of the moral whole? The answer given is that physical evil enriches the whole by giving rise to moral goodness. Disease, insanity, physical suffering and the like are said to bring into being the noble moral virtues—courage, endurance, benevolence, sympathy and the like. This is what the talk about the enriched whole comes to. W. D. Niven makes this explicit in his version of the argument:

> Physical evil has been the goad which has impelled men to most of those achievements which made the history of man so wonderful. Hardship is a stern but fecund parent of invention. Where life is easy because physical ills are at a minimum we find man degenerating in body, mind, and character.

And Niven concludes by asking:

"Which is preferable—a grim fight with the possibility of splendid triumph; or no battle at all?" [6]

The argument is: Physical evil brings moral good into being, and in fact is an essential precondition for the existence of some moral goods. Further, it is sometimes argued in this context that those moral goods which are possible in the total absence of physical evils are more valuable in themselves if they are achieved as a result of a struggle. Hence physical evil is said to be justified on the grounds that moral good plus physical evil is better than the absence of physical evil.

A common reply, and an obvious one, is that urged by Mackie.[7] Mackie argues that whilst it is true that moral good plus physical evil together are better than physical good alone, the issue is not as simple as that, for physical evil also gives rise to and makes possible many moral

---

[6] W. D. Niven, "Good and Evil," *Encyclopedia of Religion and Ethics,* James Hastings, ed., Vol. VI (New York: Charles Scribner's Sons, 1927).

Joyce's corresponding argument runs:

"Pain is the great stimulant to action. Man no less than animals is impelled to work by the sense of hunger. Experience shows that, were it not for this motive the majority of men would be content to live in indolent ease. Man must earn his bread.

"One reason plainly why God permits suffering is that man may rise to a height of heroism which would otherwise have been beyond his scope. Nor are these the only benefits which it confers. That sympathy for others which is one of the most precious parts of our experience, and one of the most fruitful sources of well-doing, has its origin in the fellow-feeling engendered by endurance of similar trials. Futhermore, were it not for these trials, man would think little enough of a future existence, and of the need of striving after his last end. He would be perfectly content with his existence, and would reck little of any higher good. These considerations here briefly advanced suffice at least to show how important is the office filled by pain in human life, and with what little reason it is asserted that the existence of so much suffering is irreconcilable with the wisdom of the Creator."

And:

"It may be asked whether the Creator could not have brought man to perfection without the use of suffering. Most certainly He could have conferred upon him a similar degree of virtue without requiring any effort on his part. Yet it is easy to see that there is a special value attaching to a conquest of difficulties such as man's actual demands, and that in God's eyes this may well be an adequate reason for assigning this life to us in preference to another. . . . Pain has value in respect to the next life, but also in respect to this. The advance of scientific discovery, the gradual improvement of the organization of the community, the growth of material civilization are due in no small degree to the stimulus afforded by pain."

[7] Mackie, "Evil and Omnipotence." (See above, pp. 46ff.)

evils that would not or could not occur in the absence of physical evil. It is then urged that it is not clear that physical evils (for example, disease and pain) plus some moral goods (for example, courage) plus some moral evil (for example, brutality) are better than physical good and those moral goods which are possible and which would occur in the absence of physical evil.

This sort of reply, however, is not completely satisfactory. The objection it raises is a sound one, but it proceeds by conceding too much to the theist, and by overlooking two more basic defects of the argument. It allows implicitly that the problem of physical evil may be reduced to the problem of moral evil; and it ngelects the two objections which show that the problem of physical evil cannot be so reduced.

The theist therefore happily accepts this kind of reply, and argues that, if he can give a satisfactory account of moral evil he will then have accounted for both physical and moral evil. He then goes on to account for moral evil in terms of the value of free will and/or its goods. This general argument is deceptively plausible. It breaks down for the two reasons indicated here, but it breaks down at another point as well. If free will alone is used to justify moral evil, then even if no moral good occurred, moral evil would still be said to be justified; but physical evil would have no justification. Physical evil is not essential to free will; it is only justified if moral good actually occurs, and if the moral good which results from physical evils outweighs the moral evils. This means that the argument from free will cannot alone justify physical evil along these lines; and it means that the argument from free will and its goods does not justify physical evil, because such an argument is incomplete, and necessarily incomplete. It needs to be supplemented by factual evidence that it is logically and practically impossible to obtain.

The correct reply, therefore, is first that the argument is irrelevant to many instances of physical evil, and secondly that it is not true that physical evil plus the moral good it produces is better than physical good and its moral goods. Much pain and suffering, in fact much physical evil generally, for example in children who die in infancy, animals and the insane passes unnoticed; it therefore has no morally uplifting effects upon others, and cannot by virtue of the examples chosen have such effects on the sufferers. Further, there are physical evils such as insanity and much disease to which the argument is inapplicable. So there is a large group of significant cases not covered by the argument. And where the argument is relevant, its premise is plainly false. It can be shown to be false by exposing its implications in the following way:

We either have obligations to lessen physical evil or we have not. If we have obligations to lessen physical evil then we are thereby reducing the total good in the universe. If, on the other hand, our obligation is to increase the total good in the universe it is our duty to prevent the reduction of physical evil and possibly even to increase the total amount of physical evil. Theists usually hold that we are obliged to reduce the physical evil in the universe; but in maintaining this, the theist is, in terms of this account of physical evil, maintaining that it is his duty to reduce the total amount of real good in the universe, and thereby to make the universe worse. Conversely, if by eliminating the physical evil he is not making the universe worse, then that amount of evil which he eliminates was unnecessary and in need of justification. It is relevant to notice here that evil is not always eliminated for morally praiseworthy reasons. Some discoveries have been due to positively unworthy motives, and many other discoveries which have resulted in a lessening of the sufferings of mankind have been due to no higher a motive than a scientist's desire to earn a reasonable living wage.

This reply to the theist's argument brings out its untenability. The theist's argument is seen to imply that war plus courage plus the many other moral virtues war brings into play are better than peace and its virtues; that famine and its moral virtues are better than plenty; that disease and its moral virtues are better than health. Some Christians in the past, in consistency with this mode of reasoning, opposed the use of anesthetics to leave scope for the virtues of endurance and courage, and they opposed state aid to the sick and needy to leave scope for the virtues of charity and sympathy. Some have even contended that war is a good in disguise, again in consistency with this argument. Similarly the theist should, in terms of this fifth argument, in his heart, if not aloud, regret the discovery of the Salk polio vaccine because Dr. Salk has in one blow destroyed infinite possibilities of moral good.

There are three important points that need to be made concerning this kind of account of physical evil. (a) We are told, as by Niven, Joyce and others, that pain is a goad to action and that part of its justification lies in this fact. This claim is empirically false as a generalization about all people and all pain. Much pain frustrates action and wrecks people and personalities. On the other hand many men work and work well without being goaded by pain or discomfort. Further, to assert that men need goading is to ascribe another evil to God, for it is to claim that God made men naturally lazy. There is no reason why God should not have made men naturally industrious; the one is no more incompatible with free will than the other. Thus the argument from physical evil being a goad to man breaks down on three distinct counts. Pain often frustrates human endeavor, pain is not essential as a goad with many men, and where pain is a goad to higher endeavors, it is clear that less evil means to this same end are available to an omnipotent God. (*b*) The real fallacy in the argument is in the assumption that all or the highest moral excellence results from physical evil. As we have already seen, this assumption is completely false. Neither all moral goodness nor the highest moral goodness is triumph in the face of adversity or benevolence towards others in suffering. Christ Himself stressed this when He observed that the two great commandments were commandments to love. Love does not depend for its possibility on the existence and conquest of evil. (*c*) The "negative" moral virtues which are brought into play by the various evils—courage, endurance, charity, sympathy and the like—besides not representing the highest forms of moral virtue, are in fact commonly supposed by the theist and atheist alike not to have the value this fifth argument ascribes to them. We —theists and atheists alike—reveal our comparative valuations of these virtues and of physical evil when we insist on state aid for the needy; when we strive for peace, for plenty, and for harmony within the state.

In brief, the good man, the morally admirable man, is he who loves what is good knowing that it is good and preferring it because it is good. He does not need to be torn by suffering or by the spectacle of another's sufferings to be morally admirable. Fortitude in his own sufferings, and sympathetic kindness in others' may reveal to us his goodness; but his goodness is not necessarily increased by such things.

Five arguments concerning physical evil have now been examined. We have seen that the problem of physical evil is a problem in its own right, and one that cannot be reduced to the problem of moral evil; and further, we have seen that physical evil creates not one but a number of problems to which no one nor any combination of the arguments examined offers a solution.

PROPOSED SOLUTIONS TO THE PROBLEM
OF MORAL EVIL

The problem of moral evil is commonly regarded as being the greater of the problems concerning evil. As we shall see, it does create what appears to be insuperable difficulties of the theist; but so too, apparently, do physical evils.

For the theist moral evil must be interpreted as a breach of God's law and as a rejection of God Himself. It may involve the eternal damnation of the sinner, and in many of its forms it involves the infliction of suffering on other persons. Thus it aggravates the problem of physical evil, but its own peculiar character consists in the fact of sin. How could a morally perfect, all-powerful God create a universe in which occur such moral evils as cruelty, cowardice and hatred, the more especially as these evils constitute a rejection of God Himself by His creations, and as such involve them in eternal damnation?

The two main solutions advanced relate to free will and to the fact that moral evil is a consequence of free will. There is a third kind of solution more often invoked implicitly than as an explicit and serious argument, which need not be examined here as its weaknesses are plainly evident. This third solution is to the effect that moral evils and even the most brutal atrocities have their justification in the moral goodness they make possible or bring into being.

1. *Free will alone provides a justification for moral evil:* This is perhaps the more popular of the serious attempts to explain moral evil. The argument in brief runs: men have free will; moral evil is a consequence of free will; a universe in which men exercise free will even with lapses into moral evil is better than a universe in which men become *automata* doing good always because predestined to do so. Thus on this argument it is the mere fact of the supreme value of free will itself that is taken to provide a justification for its corollary moral evil.

2. *The goods made possible by free will provide a basis for accounting for moral evil:* According to this second argument, it is not the mere

fact of free will that is claimed to be of such value as to provide a justification of moral evil, but the fact that free will makes certain goods
possible. Some indicate the various moral virtues as the goods that free
will makes possible, whilst others point to beatitude, and others again to
beatitude achieved by man's own efforts or the virtues achieved as a result of one's own efforts. What all these have in common is the claim
that the good consequences of free will provide a justification of the bad
consequences of free will, namely moral evil.

Each of these two proposed solutions encounters two specific criticisms,
which are fatal to their claims to be real solutions.

1. To consider first the difficulties to which the former proposed solution is exposed. (a) A difficulty for the first argument—that it is free
will alone that provides a justification for moral evil—lies in the fact
that the theist who argues in this way has to allow that it is logically
possible on the free will hypothesis that all men should always will what
is evil, and that even so, a universe of completely evil men possessing free
will is better than one in which men are predestined to virtuous living.
It has to be contended that the value of free will itself is so immense
that it more than outweighs the total moral evil, the eternal punishment
of the wicked, and the sufferings inflicted on others by the sinners in
their evilness. It is this paradox that leads to the formulation of the
second argument; and it is to be noted that the explanation of moral
evil switches to the second argument or to a combination of the first
and second argument, immediately the theist refuses to face the logical
possibility of complete wickedness, and insists instead that in fact men do
not always choose what is evil.

(b) The second difficulty encountered by the first argument relates to
the possibility that free will is compatible with less evil, and even with
no evil, that is, with absolute goodness. If it could be shown that free
will is compatible with absolute goodness, or even with less moral evil
than actually occurs, then all or at least some evil will be left unex-
plained by free will alone.

Mackie, in his recent paper, and Joyce, in his discussion of this argument, both contend that free will is compatible with absolute goodness.
Mackie argues that if it is not possible for God to confer free will on
men and at the same time ensure that no moral evil is committed He
cannot really be omnipotent. Joyce directs his argument rather to fellow-

theists, and it is more of an *ad hominem* argument addressed to them. He writes:

> Free will need not (as is often assumed) involve the power to choose wrong. Our ability to misuse the gift is due to the conditions under which it is exercised here. In our present state we are able to reject what is truly good, and exercise our power of preference in favor of some baser attraction. Yet it is not necessary that it should be so. And all who accept Christian revelation admit that those who attain their final beatitude exercise freedom of will, and yet cannot choose aught but what is truly good. They possess the knowledge of Essential Goodness; and to it, not simply to good in general, they refer every choice. Moreover, even in our present condition it is open to omnipotence so to order our circumstances and to confer on the will such instinctive impulses that we should in every election adopt the right course and not the wrong one.

To this objection, that free will is compatible with absolute goodness and that therefore a benevolent, omnipotent God would have given man free will and ensured his absolute virtue, it is replied that God is being required to perform what is logically impossible. It is logically impossible, so it is argued, for free will and absolute goodness to be combined, and hence, if God lacks omnipotence only in this respect, He cannot be claimed to lack omnipotence in any sense in which serious theists have ascribed it to Him.

Quite clearly, if free will and absolute goodness are logically incompatible, then God, in not being able to confer both on man, does not lack omnipotence in any important sense of the term. However, it is not clear that free will and absolute goodness are logically opposed; and Joyce does point to considerations which suggest that they are not logical incompatibles. For my own part I am uncertain on this point; but my uncertainty is not a factual one but one concerning a point of usage. It is clear that an omnipotent God could create rational agents predestined always to make virtuous "decisions"; what is not clear is whether we should describe such agents as having free will. The considerations to which Joyce points have something of the status of test cases, and they would suggest that we should describe such agents as having free will. However, no matter how we resolve the linguistic point, the question remains—Which is more desirable, free will and moral evil and the physical evil to which free will gives rise, or this special free will or pseudo-free will which goes with absolute goodness? I suggest that the

latter is clearly preferable. Later I shall endeavor to defend this conclusion; for the moment I am content to indicate the nature of the
value judgment on which the question turns at this point.

The second objection to the proposed solution of the problem of moral
evil in terms of free will alone, is related to the contention that free
will is compatible with less moral evil than occurs, and possibly with no
moral evil. We have seen what is involved in the latter contention. We
may now consider what is involved in the former. It may be argued
that free will is compatible with less moral evil than in fact occurs on
various grounds. (i) God, if He were all-powerful, could miraculously
intervene to prevent some or perhaps all moral evil; and He is said to
do so on occasions in answer to prayers (for example, to prevent wars)
or of His own initiative (for instance, by producing calamities which
serve as warnings, or by working miracles, etc.).

(ii) God has made man with a certain nature. This nature is often
interpreted by theologians as having a bias to evil. Clearly God could
have created man with a strong bias to good, whilst still leaving scope
for a decision to act evilly. Such a bias to good would be compatible with
freedom of the will. (iii) An omnipotent God could so have ordered the
world that it was less conducive to the practice of evil.

These are all considerations advanced by Joyce, and separately and
jointly, they establish that God could have conferred free will upon us,
and at least very considerably *reduced* the amount of moral evil that
would have resulted from the exercise of free will. This is sufficient to
show that *not all* the moral evil that exists can be justified by reference
to free will alone. This conclusion is fatal to the account of moral evil
in terms of free will alone. The more extreme conclusion that Mackie
seeks to establish—that absolute goodness is compatible with free will
—is not essential as a basis for refuting the free will argument. The
difficulty is as fatal to the claims of theism whether all moral evil or
only some moral evil is unaccountable. However, whether Mackie's
contentions are sound is still a matter of logical interest, although not of
any real moment in the context of the case against theism, once the
fact that less moral evil is compatible with free will has been established.

2. The second free will argument arises out of an attempt to circum-
vent these objections. It is not free will, but the value of the goods

achieved through free will that is said to be so great as to provide a justification for moral evil.

(a) This second argument meets a difficulty in that it is now necessary for it to be supplemented by a proof that the number of people who practice moral virtue or who attain beatitude and/or virtue after a struggle is sufficient to outweigh the evilness of moral evil, the evilness of their eternal damnation and the physical evil they cause to others. This is a serious defect in the argument, because it means that the argument can at best show that moral evil *may have* a justification, and not that it has a justification. It is both logically and practically impossible to supplement and complete the argument. It is necessarily incomplete and inconclusive even if its general principle is sound.

(b) This second argument is designed also to avoid the other difficulty of the first argument—that free will may be compatible with no evil and certainly with less evil. It is argued that even if free will is compatible with absolute goodness it is still better that virtue and beatitude be attained after a genuine personal struggle; and this, it is said, would not occur if God in conferring free will nonetheless prevented moral evil or reduced the risk of it. Joyce argues in this way:

> To receive our final beatitude as the fruit of our labors, and as the recompense of a hard-won victory, is an incomparably higher destiny than to receive it without any effort on our part. And since God in His wisdom has seen fit to give us such a lot as this, it was inevitable that man should have the power to choose wrong. We could not be called to merit the reward due to victory without being exposed to the possibility of defeat.

There are various objections which may be urged here. First, this argument implies that the more intense the struggle, the greater is the triumph and resultant good, and the better the world; hence we should apparently, on this argument, court temptation and moral struggles to attain greater virtue and to be more worthy of our reward. Secondly, it may be urged that God is being said to be demanding too high a price for the goods produced. He is omniscient. He knows that many will sin and not attain the goods or the Good free will is said to make possible. He creates men with free will, with the natures men have, in the world as it is constituted, knowing that in His doing so He is committing many to moral evil and eternal damnation. He could avoid all this evil by creating men with rational wills predestined to virtue, or He could eliminate much of it by making men's natures and the conditions in the world more conducive to the practice of virtue. He is said not to choose to do this. Instead, at the cost of the sacrifice of the many, He is said to have ordered things so as to allow fewer men to attain this higher virtue and higher beatitude that result from the more intense struggle.

In attributing such behavior to God, and in attempting to account for moral evil along these lines, theists are, I suggest, attributing to God immoral behavior of a serious kind—of a kind we should all unhesitatingly condemn in a fellow human being.

We do not commend people for putting temptation in the way of others. On the contrary, anyone who today advocated, or even allowed where he could prevent it, the occurrence of evil and the sacrifice of the many—even as a result of their own freely chosen actions—for the sake of the higher virtue of the few, would be condemned as an immoralist. To put severe temptation in the way of the many, knowing that many and perhaps even most will succumb to the temptation, for the sake of the higher virtue of the few, would be blatant immorality; and it would be immoral whether or not those who yielded to the temptation possessed free will. This point can be brought out by considering how a conscientious moral agent would answer the question: Which should I choose for other people, a world in which there are intense moral struggles and the possibility of magnificent triumphs and the certainty of many defeats, or a world in which there are less intense struggles, less magnificent triumphs but more triumphs and fewer defeats, or a world in which there are no struggles, no triumphs and no defeats? We are constantly answering less easy questions than this in a way that conflicts with the theist's contentions. If by modifying our own behavior we can save someone else from an intense moral struggle and almost certain moral evil, for example if by refraining from gambling or excessive drinking ourselves we can help a weaker person not to become a confirmed gambler or an alcoholic, or if by locking our car and not leaving it unlocked and with the key in it we can prevent people yielding to the temptation to become car thieves, we feel obliged to act accordingly, even though the persons concerned would freely choose the evil course of conduct. How much clearer is the decision with which God is said to be faced—the choice between the higher virtue of some and the evil of others, or the higher but less high virtue of many more, and the evil of many fewer. Neither alternative denies free will to men.

These various difficulties dispose of each of the main arguments relating to moral evil. There are in addition to these difficulties two other objections that might be urged.

If it could be shown that man has not free will both arguments collapse; and even if it could be shown that God's omniscience .is incompatible with free will they would still break down. The issues raised here are too great to be pursued in this paper; and they can simply be noted as possible additional grounds from which criticisms of the main proposed solutions of the problem of moral evil may be advanced.

The other general objection is by way of a follow-up to points made in objections (*b*) to both arguments (1) and (2). It concerns the relative value of free will and its goods and evils and the value of the best of the alternatives to free will and its goods. Are free will and its goods so much more valuable than the next best alternatives that their superior value can really justify the immense amount of evil that is introduced into the world by free will?

Theologians who discuss this issue ask, Which is better—men with free will striving to work out their own destinies, or automata-machinelike creatures, who never make mistakes because they never make decisions? When put in this form we naturally doubt whether free will plus moral evil plus the possibility of the eternal damnation of the many and the physical evil of untold billions are quite so unjustified after all; but the fact of the matter is that the question has not been fairly put. The real alternative is, on the one hand, rational agents with free wills making many bad and some good decisions on rational and nonrational grounds, and "rational" agents predestined always "to choose" the right things for the right reasons—that is, if the language of automata must be used, rational automata. Predestination does not imply the absence of rationality in all senses of that term. God, were He omnipotent, could preordain the decisions and the reasons upon which they were based; and such a mode of existence would seem to be in itself a worthy mode of existence, and one preferable to an existence with free will, irrationality and evil.

CONCLUSION

In this paper it has been maintained that God, were He all-powerful and perfectly good, would have created a world in which there was no unnecessary evil. It has not been argued that God ought to have created a perfect world, nor that He should have made one that is in any way logically impossible. It has simply been argued that a benevolent God could, and would, have created a world devoid of superfluous evil. It has been contended that there is evil in this world—unnecessary evil—and that the more popular and philosophically more significant of the many attempts to explain this evil are completely unsatisfactory. Hence we must conclude from the existence of evil that there cannot be an omnipotent, benevolent God.

HUME ON EVIL

NELSON PIKE

In parts **X** and **XI** of the *Dialogues Concerning Natural Religion,* Hume sets forth his views on the traditional theological problem of evil. Hume's remarks on this topic seem to me to contain a rich mixture of insight and oversight. It will be my purpose in this paper to disentangle these contrasting elements of his discussion.[1]

PHILO'S FIRST POSITION

(A) God, according to the traditional Christian view put forward by Cleanthes in the *Dialogues,* is all-powerful, all-knowing, and perfectly good. And it is clear that for Cleanthes, the terms "powerful,"

From The Philosophical Review, *Vol. LXXII, No. 2 (1963). Reprinted by permission of the editors of* The Philosophical Review.
[1] For Parts X and XI of the *Dialogues Concerning Natural Religion,* see above, pp. 17 ff.

"knowing," and "good" apply to God in exactly the same sense in which these terms apply to men. Philo argues as follows (pp. 17-25): If God is to be all-powerful, all-knowing, and perfectly good (using all key terms in their ordinary sense), then to claim that God exists is to preclude the possibility of admitting that there occur instances of evil; that is, is to preclude the possibility of admitting that there occur instances of suffering, pain, superstition, wickedness, and so forth.[2] The statements "God exists" and "There occur instances of suffering" are logically incompatible. Of course, no one could deny that there occur instances of suffering. Such a denial would plainly conflict with common experience.[3] Thus it follows from obvious fact that God (having the attributes assigned to him by Cleanthes) does not exist.

This argument against the existence of God has enjoyed considerable popularity since Hume wrote the *Dialogues*. Concerning the traditional theological problem of evil, F. H. Bradley comments as follows:

> The trouble has come from the idea that the Absolute is a moral person. If you start from that basis, then the relation of evil to the Absolute presents at once an irreducible dilemma. The problem then becomes insoluble, but not because it is obscure or in any way mysterious. To anyone who has the sense and courage to see things as they are, and is resolved not to mystify others or himself, *there is really no question to discuss. The dilemma is plainly insoluble because it is based on a clear self-contradiction.*[4]

John Stuart Mill,[5] J. E. McTaggart,[6] Antony Flew,[7] H. D. Aiken,[8]

---

[2] It is clear that, for Philo, the term "evil" is used simply as a tag for the class containing all instances of suffering, pain and so on. Philo offers no analysis of "evil" nor does his challenge to Cleanthes rest in the least on the particularities of the logic of this term. On page 25, for example, Philo formulates his challenge to Cleanthes without using "evil." Here he speaks only of *misery*. In what is to follow, I shall (following Hume) make little use of "evil." Also, I shall use "suffering" as short for "suffering pain, superstition, wickedness, and so on."

[3] Had Philo been dealing with "evil" (defined in some special way) instead of "suffering," this move in the argument might not have been open to him.

[4] *Appearance and Reality* (London: Oxford University Press, 1930), p. 174. Italics mine.

[5] *Theism* (New York: The Liberal Arts Press, 1957), p. 40. See also *The Utility of Religion* (New York: The Liberal Arts Press, 1957), pp. 73ff.

[6] *Some Dogmas of Religion* (London: Edward Arnold, Ltd., 1906), pp. 212f.

[7] "Theology and Falsification," in *New Essays in Philosophical Theology*, A. Flew and A. MacIntyre, eds. (New York: The Macmillan Company, 1955), p. 108.

[8] "God and Evil: Some Relations Between Faith and Morals," *Ethics*, Vol. LXVIII (1958). 77ff.

J. L. Mackie,[9] C. J. Ducasse,[10] and H. J. McCloskey[11] are but a very few of the many others who have echoed Philo's finalistic dismissal of traditional theism after making reference to the logical incompatibility of "God exists" and "There occur instances of suffering." W. T. Stace refers to Hume's discussion of the matter as follows:

> (Assuming that "good" and "powerful" are used in theology as they are used in ordinary discourse), we have to say that Hume was right. The charge has never been answered and never will be. The simultaneous attribution of all-power and all-goodness to the Creator of the whole world is logically incompatible with the existence of evil and pain in the world, for which reason the conception of a finite God, who is not all-powerful . . . has become popular in some quarters.[12]

In the first and second sections of this paper, I shall argue that the argument against the existence of God presented in Part X of the *Dialogues* is quite unconvincing. It is not at all clear that "God exists" and "There occur instances of suffering" are logically incompatible statements.

(B) Moving now to the details of the matter, we may, I think, formulate Philo's first challenge to Cleanthes as follows:

(1) The world contains instances of suffering.

(2) God exists—and is omnipotent and omniscient.

(3) God exists—and is perfectly good.

According to the view advanced by Philo, these three statements constitute an "inconsistent triad" (pp. 22-23). Any two of them might be held together. But if any two of them are endorsed, the third must be denied. Philo argues that to say of God that he is omnipotent and omniscient is to say that he *could* prevent suffering if he wanted to. Unless God could prevent suffering, he would not qualify as both omnipotent and omniscient. But, Philo continues, to say of God that he is perfectly good is to say that God *would* prevent suffering if he could. A being who would not prevent suffering when it was within his power to do so would not qualify as perfectly good. Thus, to affirm

---

[9] "Evil and Omnipotence." (See above, pp. 46ff.)

[10] *A Philosophical Scrutiny of Religion* (New York: The Ronald Press Company, 1953), Chap. 16.

[11] "God and Evil." (See above, pp. 61ff.)

[12] *Time and Eternity* (Princeton: Princeton University Press, 1952), p. 56.

propositions (2) and (3) is to affirm the existence of a being who both could prevent suffering if he wanted to and who would prevent suffering if he could. This, of course, is to deny the truth of proposition (1). By similar reasoning, Philo would insist, to affirm (1) and (2) is to deny the truth of (3). And to affirm (1) and (3) is to deny the truth of (2). But, as conceived by Cleanthes, God is both omnipotent-omniscient and perfectly good. Thus, as understood by Cleanthes, "God exists" and "There occur instances of suffering" are logically incompatible statements. Since the latter of these statements is obviously true, the former must be false. Philo reflects: "Nothing can shake the solidarity of this reasoning, so short, so clear (and) so decisive" (p. 25).

It seems to me that this argument it deficient. I do not think it follows from the claim that a being is perfectly good that he would prevent suffering if he could.

Consider this case. A parent forces a child to take a spoonful of bitter medicine. The parent thus brings about an instance of discomfort —suffering. The parent could have refrained from administering the medicine; and he knew that the child would suffer discomfort if he did administer it. Yet, when we are assured that the parent acted in the interest of the child's health and happiness, the fact that he knowingly caused discomfort is not sufficient to remove the parent from the class of perfectly good beings. If the parent fails to fit into this class, it is not because he caused *this* instance of suffering.

Given only that the parent knowingly caused an instance of discomfort, we are tempted to *blame* him for his action—that is, to exclude him from the class of perfectly good beings. But when the full circumstances are known, blame becomes inappropriate. In this case, there is what I shall call a "morally sufficient reason" for the parent's action. To say that there is a morally sufficient reason for his action is simply to say that there is a circumstance or condition which, when known, renders *blame* (though, of course, not *responsibility*) for the action inappropriate. As a general statement, a being who permits (or brings about) an instance of suffering might be perfectly good providing only that there is a morally sufficient reason for his action. Thus, it does not follow from the claim that God is perfectly good that he would prevent suffering if he could. God might fail to prevent suffering, or himself bring about suffering, while remaining perfectly good. It is required only that there be a morally sufficient reason for his action.

(C) In the light of these reflections, let us now attempt to put Philo's challenge to Cleanthes in sharper form.

(4) The world contains instances of suffering.

(5) God exists—and is omnipotent, omniscient, and perfectly good.

(6) An omnipotent and omniscient being would have no morally sufficient reason for allowing instances of suffering.

This sequence is logically tight. Suppose (6) and (4) true. If an omnipotent and omniscient being would have no morally sufficient reason for allowing instances of suffering, then, in a world containing such instances, either there would be no omnipotent and omniscient being or that being would be blameworthy. On either of these last alternatives, proposition (5) would be false. Thus, if (6) and (4) are true, (5) must be false. In similar fashion, suppose (6) and (5) true. If an omnipotent and omniscient being would have no morally sufficient reason for allowing suffering, then, if there existed an omnipotent and omniscient being who was also perfectly good, there would occur no suffering. Thus, if (6) and (5) are true, (4) must be false. Lastly, suppose (5) and (4) true. If there existed an omnipotent and omniscient being who was also perfectly good, then if there occurred suffering, the omnipotent and omniscient being (being also perfectly good) would have to have a morally sufficient reason for permitting it. Thus, if (5) and (4) are true, (6) must be false.

Now, according to Philo (and all others concerned), proposition (4) is surely true. And proposition (6)—well, what about proposition (6)? At this point, two observations are needed.

First, it would not serve Philo's purpose were he to argue the truth of proposition (6) by enumerating a number of reasons for permitting suffering (which might be assigned to an omnipotent and omniscient being) and then by showing that in each case the reason offered is not a morally sufficient reason (when assigned to an omnipotent and omniscient being). Philo could never claim to have examined all of the possibilities. And at any given point in the argument, Cleanthes could always claim that God's reason for permitting suffering is one which Philo has not yet considered. A retreat to unexamined reasons would remain open to Cleanthes regardless of how complete the list of examined reasons seemed to be.

Second, the position held by Philo in Part X of the *Dialogues* demands that he affirm proposition (6) as a *necessary truth*. If this is not already clear, consider the following inconsistent triad.

(7) All swans are white.

(8) Some swans are not large.

(9) All white things are large.

Suppose (9) true, but not necessarily true. Either (7) or (8) must be false. But the conjunction of (7) and (8) is not contradictory. If the conjunction of (7) and (8) were contradictory, then (9) would be necessary truth. Thus, unless (9) is a necessary truth, the conjunction of (7) and (8) is not contradictory. Note what happens to this antilogism when "colored" is substituted for "large." Now (9) becomes a necessary truth and, correspondingly, (7) and (8) become logically incompatible. The same holds for the inconsistent triad we are now considering. As already discovered, Philo holds that "There are instances of suffering" (proposition 4) and "God exists" (proposition 5) are logically incompatible. But (4) and (5) will be logically incompatible only if (6) is a necessary truth. Thus, if Philo is to argue that (4) and (5) are logically incompatible, he must be prepared to affirm (6) as a necessary truth.

We may now reconstitute Philo's challenge to the position held by Cleanthes.

Proposition (4) is obviously true. No one could deny that there occur instances of suffering. But proposition (6) is a necessary truth. An omnipotent and omniscient being would have no morally sufficient reason for allowing instances of suffering—just as a bachelor would have no wife. Thus, there exists no being who is, at once, omnipotent, omniscient, and perfectly good. Proposition (5) must be false.

(D) This is a formidable challenge to Cleanthes' position. Its strength can best be exposed by reflecting on some of the circumstances or conditions which, in ordinary life, and with respect to ordinary agents, are usually counted as morally sufficient reasons for failing to prevent (or relieve) some given instance of suffering. Let me list five such reasons.

First, consider an agent who lacked physical ability to prevent some instance of suffering. Such an agent could claim to have had a morally sufficient reason for not preventing the instance in question.

Second, consider an agent who lacked knowledge of (or the means of knowing about) a given instance of suffering. Such an agent could claim to have had a morally sufficient reason for not preventing the suffering, even if (on all other counts) he had the ability to prevent it.

Third, consider an agent who knew of an instance of suffering and had the physical ability to prevent it, but did not *realize* that he had this ability. Such an agent could usually claim to have had a morally sufficient reason for not preventing the suffering. Example: if I push the button on the wall, the torment of the man in the next room will cease. I have the physical ability to push the button. I know that the man in the next room is in pain. But I do not know that pushing the button will relieve the torment. I do not push the button and thus do not relieve the suffering.

Fourth, consider an agent who had the ability to prevent an instance of suffering, knew of the suffering, knew that he had the ability to prevent it, but did not prevent it because he believed (rightly or wrongly) that to do so would be to fail to effect some future good which would outweigh the negative value of the suffering. Such an agent might well claim to have had a morally sufficient reason for not preventing the suffering. Example: go back to the case of the parent causing discomfort by administering bitter medicine to the child.

Fifth, consider an agent who had the ability to prevent an instance of suffering, knew of the suffering, knew that he had the ability to prevent it, but failed to prevent it because to do so would have involved his preventing a prior good which outweighed the negative value of the suffering. Such an agent might claim to have had a morally sufficient reason for not preventing the suffering. Example: a parent permits a child to eat some birthday cake knowing that his eating the cake will result in the child's feeling slightly ill later in the day. The parent estimates that the child's pleasure of the moment outweighs the discomfort which will result.

Up to this point, Philo would insist, we have not hit on a circumstance or condition which could be used by Cleanthes when constructing a "theodicy," that is, when attempting to identify the morally sufficient reason God has for permitting instances of suffering.

The first three entries on the list are obviously not available. Each makes explicit mention of some lack of knowledge or power on the part of the agent. Nothing more need be said about them.

A theologian might, however, be tempted to use a reason for the fourth type when constructing a theodicy. He might propose that suffering *results in goods* which outweigh the negative value of the suffering. Famine (hunger) leads man to industry and progress. Disease (pain) leads man to knowledge and understanding. Philo suggests that no theodicy of this kind can be successful (pp. 29-31). An omnipotent and omniscient being could find other means of bringing about the same results. The mere fact that evils give rise to goods cannot serve as a morally sufficient reason for an omnipotent and omniscient being to permit suffering.

A theologian might also be tempted to use reasons of the fifth type when constructing a theodicy. He might propose that instances of suffering *result from goods* which outweigh the negative value of the suffering. That the world is run in accordance with natural law is good. But any such regular operation will result in suffering. That men have the ability to make free choices is good. But free choice will sometimes result in wrong choice and suffering. Philo argues that it is not at all clear that a world run in accordance with natural law is better than one not so regulated (p. 29). And one might issue a similar challenge with respect to free will. But a more general argument has been offered in the contemporary literature on evil which is exactly analogous to the one suggested by Philo above. According to H. J. McCloskey, an omnipotent and omniscient being could devise a law-governed world which would not include suffering.[13] And according to J. L. Mackie, an omnipotent and omniscient being could create a world containing free agents which would include no suffering or wrong-doing.[14] The import of both of these suggestions is that an omnipotent and omniscient being could create a world containing whatever is good (regularity, free will, and so on) without allowing the suffering which (only factually) results from these goods. The mere fact that suffering results

[13] "God and Evil." (See above, pp. 69f.)
[14] "Evil and Omnipotence." (See above, pp. 56f.)

from good cannot serve as a morally sufficient reason for an omnipotent and omniscient being to allow suffering.

Though the above reflections may be far from conclusive, let us grant that, of the morally sufficient reasons so far considered, none could be assigned to an omnipotent and omniscient being. This, of course, is not to say that proposition (6) is true—let alone necessarily true. As mentioned earlier, proposition (6) will not be shown true by an enumerative procedure of the above kind. But consider the matter less rigorously. If none of the reasons so far considered could be assigned to an omnipotent and omniscient being, ought this not to raise a suspicion? Might there not be a principle operating in each of these reasons which guarantees that *no* morally sufficient reason for permitting suffering *could* be assigned to an omnipotent and omniscient being? Such a principle immediately suggests itself. Men are sometimes excused for allowing suffering. But in these cases, men are excused only because they lack the knowledge or power to prevent suffering, or because they lack the knowledge or power to bring about goods (which are causally related to suffering) without also bringing about suffering. In other words, men are excusable only because they are limited. Having a morally sufficient reason for permitting suffering *entails* having some lack of knowledge or power. If this principle is sound (and, indeed, it is initially plausible) then proposition (6) must surely be listed as a necessary truth.

DEMEA'S THEODICY

But the issue is not yet decided. Demea has offered a theodicy which does not fit any of the forms outlined above. And Philo must be willing to consider all proposals if he is to claim "decisiveness" for his argument against Cleanthes.

Demea reasons as follows:

This world is but a point in comparison of the universe; this life but a moment in comparison of eternity. The present evil phenomena, therefore, are rectified in other regions, and in some future period of existence. And the eyes of men, being then opened to larger views of things, see the whole connection of general laws, and trace, with adoration, the benevolence and rectitude of the Deity through all mazes and intricacies of his providence [p. 24].

It might be useful if we had a second statement of this theodicy, one taken from a traditional theological source. In Chapter LXXI of the *Summa Contra Gentiles,* St. Thomas argues as follows:

> The good of the whole is of more account than the good of the part. Therefore, it belongs to a prudent governor to overlook a lack of goodness in a part, that there may be an increase of goodness in the whole. Thus, the builder hides the foundation of a house underground, that the whole house may stand firm. Now, if evil were taken away from certain parts of the universe, the perfection of the universe would be much diminished, since its beauty results from the ordered unity of good and evil things, seeing that evil arises from the failure of good, and yet certain goods are occasioned from those very evils through the providence of the governor, even as the silent pause gives sweetness to the chant. Therefore, evil should not be excluded from things by the divine providence.

Neither of these statements seems entirely satisfactory. Demea might be suggesting that the world is good on the whole—that the suffering we discover in our world is, as it were, made up for in other regions of creation. God here appears as the husband who beats his wife on occasion but makes up for it with favors at other times. In St. Thomas' statement, there are unmistakable hints of causal reasoning. Certain goods are "occasioned" by evils, as the foundation of the house permits the house to stand firm. But in both of these statements another theme is at least suggested. Let me state and expand it in my own way without pretense of historical accuracy.

I have a set of ten wooden blocks. There is a T-shaped block, an L-shaped block, an F-shaped block, and so on. No two blocks have the same shape. Let us assign each block a value—say an aesthetic value—making the T-shaped block most valuable and the L-shaped block least valuable. Now the blocks may be fitted together into formations. And let us suppose that the blocks are so shaped that there is one and only one subset of the blocks which will fit together into a square. The L-shaped block is a member of that subset. Further, let us stipulate that any formation of blocks (consisting of two or more blocks fitted together) will have more aesthetic value than any of the blocks taken individually or any subset of the blocks taken as a mere collection. And, as a last assumption, let us say that the square formation has greater aesthetic value than any other logically possible block formation. The

L-shaped block is a necessary component of the square formation; that is, the L-shaped block is logically indispensable to the square formation. Thus the L-shaped block is a necessary component of the best of all possible block formations. Hence, the block with the least aesthetic value is logically indispensable to the best of all possible block formations. Without this very block, it would be logically impossible to create the best of all possible block formations.

Working from this model, let us understand Demea's theodicy as follows. Put aside the claim that instances of suffering are *de facto* causes or consequences of greater goods. God, being a perfectly good, omniscient, and omnipotent being, would create the best of all possible worlds. But the best of all possible worlds must contain instances of suffering: they are logically indispensable components. This is why there are instances of suffering in the world which God created.

What shall we say about this theodicy? Philo expresses no opinion on the subject.

Consider this reply to Demea's reasonings. A world containing instances of suffering as necessary components might be the best of all possible worlds. And if a world containing instances of suffering as necessary components were the best of all possible worlds, an omnipotent and omniscient being would have a morally sufficient reason for permitting instances of suffering. But how are we to know that, in fact, instances of suffering are logically indispensable components of the best of all possible worlds? There would appear to be no way of establishing this claim short of assuming that God does in fact exist and then concluding (as did Leibniz) that the world (containing suffering) which he did in fact create is the best of all possible worlds. But, this procedure assumes that God exists. And this latter is precisely the question now at issue.

It seems to me that this reply to Demea's theodicy has considerable merit. First, my hypothetical objector is probably right in suggesting that the only way one could show that the best of all possible worlds must contain instances of suffering would be via the above argument in which the existence of God is assumed. Second, I think my objector is right in allowing that if instances of suffering were logically indispensable components of the best of all possible worlds, this would provide a morally sufficient reason for an omnipotent and omniscient being to permit instances of suffering. And, third, I think that my objector exhibits considerable discretion in not challenging the claim that the best of all possible worlds *might* contain instances of suffering as necessary components. I know of no argument which will show this claim to be true. But on the other hand, I know of no argument which will show this claim to be false. (I shall elaborate this last point directly.)

Thus, as I have said, the above evaluation of the theodicy advanced by Demea seems to have considerable merit. But this evaluation, *if correct,* seems to be sufficient to refute Philo's claim that "God exists" and "There occur instances of suffering" are logically incompatible statements. If instances of suffering were necessary components of the best of all possible worlds, then an omnipotent and omniscient being would have a morally sufficient reason for permitting instances of suffering. Thus, if it is *possible* that instances of suffering are necessary components of the best of all possible worlds, then there *might be* a morally sufficient reason for an omnipotent and omniscient being to permit instances of suffering. Thus if the statement "Instances of suffering are necessary components of the best of all possible worlds" is not contradictory, then proposition (6) is not a necessary truth. And, as we have seen, if proposition (6) is not a necessary truth, then "God exists" and "There occur instances of suffering" are not logically incompatible statements.

What shall we say? Is the statement "Instances of suffering are logically indispensable components of the best of all possible worlds" contradictory? That it is is simply assumed in Philo's first position. But, surely, this in not a trivial assumption. If it is correct, it must be shown to be so; it is not *obviously* correct. And how shall we argue that it is correct? Shall we, for example, assume that any case of suffering contained in any complex of events detracts from the value of the complex? If this principle were analytic, then a world containing an instance of suffering could not be the best of all possible worlds. But G. E. Moore has taught us to be suspicious of any such principle.[15] And John Wisdom has provided a series of counterexamples which tend to show that this very principle is, in fact, not analytic. Example:

---

[15] I refer here to Moore's discussion of "organic unities" in *Principia Ethica* (London: Macmillan & Co., Ltd., 1903), pp. 28ff.

if I believe (rightly or wrongly) that you are in pain and become unhappy as a result of that belief, the resulting complex would appear to be better by virtue of my unhappiness (suffering) than it would have been had I believed you to be in pain but had not become unhappy (or had become happy) as a result.[16] Philo's argument against the existence of God is not finished. And it is not at all obvious that it is *capable* of effective completion. It is, I submit, far from clear that God and evil could not exist together in the same universe.

PHILO'S SECOND POSITION

At the end of Part X, Philo agrees to "retire" from his first position. He now concedes that "God exists" and "There occur instances of suffering" are not logically incompatible statements (pp. 25ff.). (It is clear from the context that this adjustment in Philo's thinking is made only for purposes of argument and not because Hume senses any inadequacy in Philo's first position.) Most contemporary philosophers think that Hume's major contribution to the literature on evil was made in Part X of the *Dialogues*. But it seems to me that what is of really lasting value in Hume's reflections on this subject is to be found not in Part X, but in the discussion in Part XI which follows Philo's "retirement" from his first position.

(A) Consider, first of all, a theology in which the existence of God is accepted on the basis of what is taken to be a conclusive (a priori) demonstration. (A theology in which the existence of God is taken as an item of faith can be considered here as well.) On this view, that God exists is a settled matter, not subject to review or challenge. It is, as it were, axiomatic to further theological debate. According to Philo, evil in the world presents no special problem for a theology of this sort:

> Let us allow that, if the goodness of the Deity (I mean a goodness like the human) could be established on any tolerable reasons a priori, these (evil) phenomena, however untoward, would not be sufficient to subvert that principle, but might easily, in some unknown manner, be reconcilable to it [p. 33].

This point, I think, is essentially correct, but it must be put more firmly.

---

[16] "God and Evil," *Mind,* Vol. XLIV (1935), 13f. I have modified Wisdom's example slightly.

Recalling the remarks advanced when discussing the inconsistent nature of propositions (4) through (6) above, a theologian who accepts the existence of God (either as an item of faith or on the basis of an a priori argument) must conclude either that there is some morally sufficient reason for God's allowing suffering in the world, or that there are no instances of suffering in the world. He will, of course, choose the first alternative. Thus, in a theology of the sort now under consideration, the theologian begins by affirming the existence of God and by acknowledging the occurrence of suffering. It follows *logically* that God has some morally sufficient reason for allowing instances of suffering. The conclusion is not, as Philo suggests, that there *might be* a morally sufficient reason for evil. The conclusion is, rather, that there *must be* such a reason. It *could* not be otherwise.

What then of the traditional theological problem of evil? Within a theology of the above type, the problem of evil can only be the problem of discovering a *specific* theodicy which is adequate—that is, of discovering which, if any, of the specific proposals which might be advanced really describes God's morally sufficient reason for allowing instances of suffering. This problem, of course, is not a major one for the theologian. If the problem of evil is simply the problem of uncovering the specific reason for evil—given assurance that there is (and must be) some such reason—it can hardly be counted as a critical problem. Once it is granted that there is some specific reason for evil, there is a sense in which it is no longer vital to find it. A theologian of the type we are now considering might never arrive at a satisfactory theodicy. (Philo's "unknown" reason might remain forever unknown.) He might condemn as erroneous all existing theodices and might despair of ever discovering the morally sufficient reason in question. A charge of incompleteness would be the worst that could be leveled at his world view.

(B) Cleanthes is not, of course, a theologian of the sort just described. He does not accept the existence of God as an item of faith, nor on the basis of an a priori argument. In the *Dialogues,* Cleanthes supports his theological position with an a posteriori argument from design. He argues that "order" in the universe provides sufficient evidenc that the world was created by an omnipotent, omniscient, and perfectly good being.[17] He proposes the existence of God as a quasi-scientific explanatory hypothesis, arguing its truth via the claim that it provides an adequate explanation for observed facts.

Philo has two comments to make regarding the relevance of suffering in the world for a theology of this kind.

The first is a comment with which Philo is obviously well pleased. It is offered at the end of Part X and is repeated no less than three times in Part XI. It is this: even if the existence of God and the occurrence of suffering in the world are logically compatible, one cannot argue from a world containing suffering to the existence of an omnipotent, omniscient, and perfectly good creator. This observation, I think all would agree, is correct. Given only a painting containing vast areas of green, one could not effectively argue that its creator disliked using green. There would be no *logical* conflict in holding that a painter who disliked using green painted a picture containing vast areas of green. But given *only* the picture (and no further information), the hypothesis that its creator disliked using green would be poorly supported indeed.

It is clear that in this first comment Philo has offered a criticism of Cleanthes' *argument* for the existence of God. He explicitly says that this complaint is against Cleanthes' *inference* from a world containing instances of suffering to the existence of an omnipotent, omniscient, and perfectly good creator (pp. 27-28). Philo's second comment, however, is more forceful than this. It is a challenge of the *truth* of Cleanthes' *hypothesis.*

Philo argues as follows:

Look round this universe. What an immense profusion of beings, animated and organized, sensible and active! You admire this prodigious variety and fecundity. But inspect a little more narrowly these living existences, the only beings worth regarding. How

---

[17] It is interesting to notice that, in many cases, theologians who have used an argument from design have not attempted to argue that "order" in the world proves the existence of a perfectly moral being. For example, in St. Thomas' "fifth way" and in William Paley's *Natural Theology,* "order" is used to show only that the creator of the world was *intelligent.* There are, however, historical instances of the argument from design being used to prove the goodness as well as the intelligence of a creator. For example, Bishop Berkeley argues this way in the second of the *Dialogues Between Hylas and Philonous.*

hostile and destructive to each other! How insufficient all of them for their own happiness! . . . There is indeed an opposition of pains and pleasures in the feelings of sensible creatures; but are not all the operations of nature carried on by an opposition of principles, of hot and cold, moist and dry, light and heavy! The true conclusion is that the original Source of all things is entirely indifferent to all these principles, and has no more regard to good above ill than to heat above cold, or to drought above moisture, or to light above heavy [p. 34].

Philo claims that *there is* an "original Source of all things" and that this source is indifferent with respect to matters of good and evil. He pretends to be inferring this conclusion from observed data. This represents a departure from Philo's much professed skepticism in the *Dialogues.* And, no doubt, many of the criticisms of Cleanthes' position which Philo advanced earlier in the *Dialogues* would apply with equal force to the inference Philo has just offered. But I shall not dwell on this last point. I think the center of Philo's remarks in this passage must be located in their skeptical rather than their metaphysical import. Philo has proposed a hypothesis which is counter to the one offered by Cleanthes. And he claims that his hypothesis is the "true conclusion" to be drawn from the observed data. But the point is not, I think, that Philo's new hypothesis is true, or even probable. The conclusion is, rather, that the hypothesis advanced by Cleanthes is false, or very improbable. When claiming that evil in the world *supports* a hypothesis which is counter to the one offered by Cleanthes, I think Philo simply means to be calling attention to the fact that evil in the world provides *evidence against* Cleanthes' theological position.

Consider the following analogy which, I think, will help expose this point. I am given certain astronomical data. In order to explain the data, I introduce the hypothesis that there exists a planet which has not yet been observed but will be observable at such and such a place in the sky at such and such a time. No other hypothesis seems as good. The anticipated hour arrives and the telescopes are trained on the designated area. No planet appears. Now, either one of two conclusions may be drawn. First, I might conclude that there is no planet there to be seen. This requires either that I reject the original astronomical data or that I admit that what seemed the best explanation of the data is not, in fact, the true explanation. Second, I might conclude that there is a planet there to be seen, but that something in the observational set-up went amiss. Perhaps the equipment was faulty, perhaps there were clouds, and so on. Which conclusion is correct? The answer is not straightforward. I must check both possibilities.

Suppose I find nothing in the observational set-up which is in the least out of order. My equipment is in good working condition, I find no clouds, and so on. To decide to retain the planet hypothesis in the face of the recalcitrant datum (my failure to observe the planet) is, in part, to decide that there is some circumstance (as yet unknown) which explains the datum *other* than the nonexistence of the planet in question. But a decision to retain the planet hypothesis (in the face of my failure to observe the planet and in the absence of an explicit explanation which "squares" this failure with the planet hypothesis) is made correctly *only* when the *evidence for* the planet hypothesis is such as to render its negation less plausible than would be the assumption of a (as yet unknown) circumstance which explains the observation failure. This, I think, is part of the very notion of dealing reasonably with an explanatory hypothesis.

Now Cleanthes has introduced the claim that there exists an omnipotent, omniscient, and perfectly good being as a way of explaining "order" in the world. And Philo, throughout the *Dialogues* (up to and including most of Part XI), has been concerned to show that this procedure provides very little (if any) solid evidence for the existence of God. The inference from the data to the hypothesis is extremely tenuous. Philo is now set for his final thrust at Cleanthes' position. Granting that God and evil are not logically incompatible, the existence of human suffering in the world must still be taken as a recalcitrant datum with respect to Cleanthes' hypothesis. Suffering, as Philo says, is not what we should antecedently expect in a world created by an omnipotent, omniscient, and perfectly good being (pp. 27-28). Since Cleanthes has offered nothing in the way of an explicit theodicy (that is, an explanation of the recalcitrant datum which would "square" it with his hypothesis) and since the *evidence for* his hypothesis is extremely weak and generally ineffective, there is pretty good reason for thinking that Cleanthes' hypothesis is false.

This, I think, is the skeptical import of Philo's closing remarks in Part XI. On this reading nothing is said about an "original Source of all things" which is indifferent with respect to matters of good and evil. Philo is simply making clear the negative force of the fact of evil in the world for a hypothesis such as the one offered by Cleanthes.

It ought not to go unnoticed that Philo's closing attack on Cleanthes' position has extremely limited application. Evil in the world has central negative importance for theology only when theology is approached as a quasi-scientific subject, as by Cleanthes. That it is seldom approached in this way will be evident to anyone who has studied the history of theology. Within most theological positions, the existence of God is taken as an item of faith or embraced on the basis of an a priori argument. Under these circumstances, where there is nothing to qualify as a "hypothesis" capable of having either negative or positive "evidence," the fact of evil in the world presents no special problem for theology. As Philo himself has suggested, when the existence of God is accepted prior to any rational consideration of the status of evil in the world, the traditional problem of evil reduces to a noncrucial perplexity of relatively minor importance.

OMNIPOTENCE, EVIL

AND SUPERMEN

NINIAN SMART

It has in recent years been argued, by Professors Antony Flew and J. L. Mackie;[1] that God could have created men wholly good. For, causal determinism being compatible with free will, men could have been made in such a way that, without loss of freedom, they would never have fallen (and would never fall) into sin. This if true would constitute a weighty antitheistic argument. And yet intuitively it seems unconvincing. I wish here to uncover the roots of this intuitive suspicion.

There are in the argument two assertions to be distinguished. First, that causal determinism (i.e., the claim that all human actions are the results of prior causes) is compatible with free will.[2] I call this the Compatibility Thesis. Second, there is the assertion that God could have

---

From Philosophy, *Vol. XXXVI, No. 137 (1961). Reprinted by permission of the author and the editors of* Philosophy.

[1] See Antony Flew, "Divine Omnipotence and Human Freedom," in *New Essays in Philosophical Theology,* A. Flew and A. MacIntyre, eds. (New York: The Macmillan Company, 1955), Chap. 8, and J. L. Mackie, "Evil and Omnipotence." (See above, pp. 46ff.)

[2] See Flew, *op. cit.,* p. 151.

created men wholly good. This I shall call the Utopia Thesis. An apparent inference from the latter is that God cannot be both omnipotent and wholly good, since men are in fact wicked.

In the present discussion I shall concentrate on the Utopia Thesis. Clearly, of course, if the Compatibility Thesis is not established the Utopia Thesis loses its principal basis and becomes altogether doubtful. But I shall here merely try to show that the Utopia Thesis does not follow from the Compatibility Thesis, despite appearances. This may well indicate that there is something queer about the latter (and the Paradigm Case Argument, on which perhaps it principally rests, has lately come in for perspicacious criticisms).[3] In the discussion I shall be assuming the truth of determinism; for if it is false, the Compatibility Thesis becomes irrelevant and the Utopia Thesis totters. The chief points in my reasoning are as follows:

The concept *good* as applied to humans connects with other concepts such as *temptation, courage, generosity,* etc. These concepts have no clear application if men were built wholly good. I bring this out by a piece of anthropological fiction, i.e., (1) let us conjure up a universe like ours, only where men are supposed to be wholly good; or (2) let us consider the possibility of Utopian universes quite unlike ours. Under (1), I try to show that it is unclear whether the "men" in such a universe are to be called wholly good or even good, and that it is unclear whether they should be called men. And under (2), I try to show that we have even stronger reasons for saying that these things are unclear. Thus the abstract possibility that men might have been created wholly good has no clearly assignable content. Hence, it is rational to be quite agnostic about such a possibility. It follows that it will be quite unclear whether a Utopian universe will be superior (in respect of moral goodness) to ours. So the Utopia Thesis cannot constitute an antitheistic argument.

I

When we say that a man is good, we are liable to render an account of why we say this by giving reasons. For example, it might be because

---

[3] See the article "Farewell to the Paradigm-Case Argument" by J. W. N. Watkins, and Flew's comment and Watkins' reply to the comment, all in *Analysis*, Vol. XVIII, No. 2 (1957), and the articles by R. Harré and H. G. Alexander in *Analysis*, Vol. XVIII, Nos. 4-5 (1958), respectively.

he has been heroic in resisting temptations, courageous in the face of difficulties, generous to his friends, etc. Thus *good* normally connects with concepts like *courage* and so forth.

Let us look first at *temptation*. It is clear (at least on the determinist assumption) that if two identical twins were in otherwise similar situations but where one has a temptation not to do what is right, while no such temptation is presented to the other twin, and other things being equal, the tempted twin will be less likely to do what is right than the untempted one. It is this fact that temptations are empirically discovered to affect conduct that doubtless makes it relevant to consider them when appraising character and encouraging virtue. Moreover, unless we were built in a certain way there would be no temptations: for example, unless we were built so that sexual gratification is normally very pleasant there would be no serious temptations to commit adultery, etc. It would appear then that the only way to ensure that people were wholly good would be to build them in such a way that they were never tempted or only tempted to a negligible extent. True, there are two other peculiar possibilities, which I shall go on to deal with, namely (1) through lucky combination of circumstances men might never sin; (2) frequent miraculous intervention might keep them on the straight and narrow path. However, for the moment, I consider the main possibility, that to ensure that *all* men were *always* good, men would have to possess a built-in resistance to all temptations.

Similar remarks apply to courage, generosity, etc., although in some cases the situation may be rather complex. It will, I think, be conceded that we credit people with courage on such grounds as that they have faced adverse situations with calm and disregard for danger. But the adversities arise because there are fears, desires for comfort, disinclinations to offend people, and so on. And it will be generally agreed, at least by determinists, that one twin faced with a situation where doing right inspires fear will be less likely to do what is right than the other twin not so faced with adversity, and similarly with regard to desires for comfort and so forth. Thus to ensure that men would never panic, never wilt, etc., it would be necessary, as the main possibility, to build them differently.

Perhaps generosity is a trickier case. But it is clear that a person is praised for generosity because very often there is a conflict of generosity and self-interest. Indeed, if there were not some such conflict, or thought to be, however remote, an action would not really count as generosity, perhaps; the slight qualification here is due to the possibility of situations where a person has so much money, say, that it makes no psychological difference whether he gives away a certain sum or not, but he does it out of sympathy—I shall deal with such cases below. And to say that generosity conflicts with self-interest is a shorthand way of saying that one's inclinations for comfort, etc., are liable to have a more restricted fulfilment than would otherwise be the case.

Then there are actions which exhibit such dispositions as pride, which seem remote from simple inclinations such as likings for certain sorts of food or for sexual gratification and from fairly simple impulses such as fear. But though the springs of pride are hard to fathom, it is doubtless true that people would not display pride, in the ordinary sense, if they did not live in a socially competitive atmosphere, if they did not have desires to assert themselves, etc. One would not be sure quite how men would have to be rebuilt to immunize them from pride, but rebuilding would surely be necessary, on the determinist view.

As for the peculiar cases mentioned above—generosity not involving sacrifice and similar examples—I do not think that such instances are at all serious ones, inasmuch as (1) virtues are dispositions, and so there is a point in calling such nonsacrificial generosity generosity, in that it exhibits a disposition whose basic exercise involves sacrifice; (2) without the occasions for basic exercise of the disposition it is obscure as to what could be meant by calling the nonbasic instances of generosity instances of generosity.

These examples, then, are meant to indicate that the concept *goodness* is applied to beings of a certain sort, beings who are liable to temptations, possess inclinations, have fears, tend to assert themselves and so forth; and that if they were to be immunized from evil they would have to be built in a different way. But it soon becomes apparent that to rebuild them would mean that the ascription of goodness would become unintelligible, for the reasons why men are called good and bad have a connection with human nature as it is empirically discovered to be. Moral utterance is embedded in the cosmic status quo.

II

Of course, God is not bound by synthetic necessities: He is in no way shackled by the causal laws of our universe, for example. But in a back-handed way, He is confined by meaninglessness. For to say that God might do such-and-such where the "such-and-such" is meaningless or completely obscure is not to assert that God can *do* anything. I there-fore hope to show that "God might have created men wholly good" is without intelligible content, and hence that this alleged possibility has no force as an antitheistic argument.

"God might have created men wholly good" *appears* to have content because at least it does not seem self-contradictory and because we think we can imagine such a situation. But I shall bring out its emptiness by in fact trying to do this, by imagining other possible universes. Now it may well be objected that in doing this I am showing nothing. For ex-ample, one will be wanting to make imaginative causal inferences like "If men are never to panic they must be built in such-and-such a way." But since God is not bound by causal principles the inferences have no legitimacy.

But this objection misses the point of my procedure. For my argument is based on the following dilemma. *Either* we can hope to assign a rea-sonably clear meaning to the possibility that men might have been created wholly good by imagining a Utopia—in which case the paradox arises that it would be quite unclear as to whether such "men" could reason-ably be called wholly good. *Or* we can refuse to assign such a reasonably clear meaning to the possibility by simply postulating an unimaginable alternative universe—in which case there are even stronger reasons for doubting whether the possibility has content. Or, to make the matter *ad hominem* as against Flew, I am saying that alleged possibilities as well as alleged facts can die the Death by a Thousand Qualifications.

I proceed then to imagine possible universes. In line with the above dilemma, I divide such universes into two classes. First, those which are cosmomorphic, i.e., those which are governed by physical laws at least roughly comparable to those found in our cosmos. Second, I consider noncosmomorphic universes, i.e. ones with a quite different set-up from ours.

1. *Cosmomorphic Utopia A*—The first and main type of cosmomorphic utopia, where men are wholly good, can be described perhaps as follows, in line with the earlier remarks about temptation, etc.

Men will never be seriously tempted to harm or injure each other. For this reason: that no one has any serious desires liable to conflict with those of others. For instance, they would be so built that one and only one woman would attract any one man and conversely. Say: one would have an overriding infatuation for the first uninfatuated woman one met and vice versa. As for property: men might arrive in the world with an automatic supply of necessities and comforts, and the individual would have a built-in mechanism to ensure that the supplies of others were mysteriously distasteful (the other man's passion-fruit smells like dung). And what of danger? During, say, a thunderstorm no one would be so seriously perturbed that he would be likely to panic and harm others. Let us suppose that a signal would (so to speak) flash in the individual's brain, telling him to take cover. What if he was in the middle of an *al fresco* dinner? Perhaps the signal flashing would dry up the juices in his mouth. And so forth. (Admittedly this picture is not elaborated with much scientific expertize: of this I shall say more later.)

I think that none of the usual reasons for calling men good would apply in such a Utopia. Consider one of these harmless beings. He is wholly good, you say? Really? Has he been courageous? No, you reply, not exactly, for such creatures do not feel fear. Then he is generous to his friends perhaps? Not precisely, you respond, for there is no question of his being ungenerous. Has he resisted temptations? No, not really, for there are no temptations (nothing you could really *call* temptations). Then why call them good? Well, you say, these creatures never harm each other. . . . Yes, but the inhabitants of Alpha Centauri never harm *us*. Ah, you reply, Centaurians do not harm us because there are as yet no ways for them to impinge upon us. Quite so, I say; it is causally impossible for them to harm us. Similarly the set-up of the Cosmomorphic Utopians makes it causally impossible for them to harm each other. The fact that it is distance in the one case and inner structure in the other makes no odds.

Now admittedly in such a conversation we are not brought face to face with the Death by a Thousand Qualifications in the form described by Flew in regard to such statements as "God loves His children." For there the criticism of the theologian is that when counterevidence is presented he takes refuge in increasingly recondite senses of "love." But in the present case one who claims that the inhabitants of Cosmomorphic Utopia A are wholly good is not precisely resisting counterevidence (that is, he is not resisting evidence that these creatures are not good and so possibly bad). Rather he is failing to give the usual reasons for calling them bad. And the positive moves are up to him. It is not sufficient airily and vaguely to say that in such an alternative universe men can be said to be wholly good. Similarly the traveller from Jupiter who tells us that unicorns are to be found there, though queer unicorns for they possess neither horns nor feet, leaves us at a justifiable loss.

Hence it is so far obscure as to what is meant by the possibility that men might have been created wholly good. For the usual criteria, at least in Cosmomorphic Utopia A, do not seem to apply. And so, even if the Compatibility Thesis is correct, it does not appear so far evident that men might have been created wholly good. For an unintelligible assertion cannot either be said to follow or not to follow from some other. And in any case, are the Utopians described above properly to be called *men?* Perhaps we ought to invent a new name: let us dub them "sapients." The question for the theist now becomes: "Why did God create men rather than sapients?" I shall return to this question later.

2. *Cosmomorphic Utopia B*—Circumstances here combine always to make men good. Adolf Hitler would never in fact be foul. He might have incipient impulses of hatred towards Jews, but these would luckily never overwhelm him, because circumstances would prevent this: he would fall in love with a Jewess, he would never get into anti-Semitic company, he would not meet with miseries in his youth, and so forth. Whenever on the point of falling for some temptation, his attention would be distracted. The whole thing would be a very, very long story. And everyone, not just the Führer, would be consistently lucky with regard to virtue and vice.

The trouble about this Utopia is that it is more like a dream than a fantasy. A corresponding meteorological dream would be: since circumstances occasionally combine to make the sun shine, let us suppose that the sky would never be overcast. This does not seem self-contradictory, to say "The sky might never be overcast." But what would a cosmomorphic universe have to be like for this to happen? Clearly it is not just luck that makes the sun shine sometimes: it is because the weather operates in a certain way. For the weather so to operate that it was never cloudy meteorological laws would have to be rewritten (and physics and biology too)—unless you are thinking of a place like the moon. Similarly, in a cosmomorphic utopia where circumstances for ever combined in favor of virtue, the set-up would, according to the determinist, have to be different. Thus Cosmomorphic Utopia B is either a version of A (or of some other) or it is a mere dream masquerading as an alternative universe.

3. *Cosmomorphic Utopia C*—Suppose men were always virtuous, not because of the set-up (which would be as now) but because of frequent miraculous intervention.

It is hard to make sense of the supposition. But observationally in such a world we might discover situations like this. Causal factors C usually give rise to actions of a certain empirical type, type-A. But in some circumstances type-A actions are wrong, and in these cases C will not have type-A effects. But it will not be that some other empirical factor will be present in such exceptions, for *ex hypothesi* the nonoccurrence of the type-A action is due to miraculous intervention. Hence either we have to count rightness and wrongness as empirical differences in order to formulate a causal law here or we must confess that no strict causal laws of human behavior could be formulated in this cosmos. The former alternative is baffling and unacceptable, while the latter is incompatible with determinism. Hence Cosmomorphic Utopia C provides no support for the Utopia Thesis.

4. I now turn to the thought of a *Noncosmomorphic Utopia*. As has been insisted, God is not limited to a cosmomorphic alternative. My anthropological fictions are feeble in comparison with the possibilities contained in God's thoughts. He might have produced a cosmos utterly unlike ours.

But as we have no notion what sapients in such a world would be like, it is even unclearer in this case what would be meant by calling them good. We would have to remain completely agnostic about such a world; and all the difficulties there are in knowing what is meant by calling God a person and good would recur with *extra* force when we try to understand what "wholly good men" could mean here. *Extra* force, because whereas God's nature is perhaps revealed to a limited extent in the *actual* cosmos, the nature of an alternative *possible* and *noncosmomorphic* universe can in no way be so revealed. Hence it follows that it is totally unclear what the possibility that God might have created a noncosmomorphic utopia amounts to.

It is therefore also unclear as to whether it would be superior to this universe. Moreover, it is most doubtful as to whether the sapients of Cosmomorphic Utopia A are superior to ourselves. I am not sure, of course, how one judges such matters; but if we rely on native wit, in default of some new method of evaluating alternative universes, it seems by no means clear that such a utopia is a better place than ours here.

III

It may be complained that I have been unfair. My anthropological fiction has been crude and possibly biased. And the thing has not been worked out with any scientific expertize. But no one, so far as I know, with the requisite physiological, psychological and biological knowledge has attempted to work out such a fictional alternative anthropology, doubtless there are enough problems in the real-life biological sciences without our going off into subtle fantasies. But until someone were to do so, it remains obscure as to what a determinist cosmomorphic utopia would amount to.

Again it may be objected that writers have occasionally dreamed of utopias and described them. Surely these descriptions are not empty or self-contradictory? But first, fictions are no good guide unless systematically elaborated. For example, and notoriously, there are situations in science fiction which are revealed on reflection to be unintelligible or self-contradictory (e.g., in regard to "going back in time"). Again, fiction writers may not have any clearly formulated views about determinism. And it might turn out that what is allowable on a hard free will theory is not so on a determinist view. For example, an indeterminist may simply say that it might have been the case that men were always wholly good. But the determinist can only make sense of this possibility on the assumption that wholly good men would have a causal difference from men as they are. In order to imagine a man's always overcoming his harmful inclinations, he must surely imagine some change in the way his personality is built. But we have no assurance that some *unspecified* causal change would leave men more or less human and yet produce the consequence of complete goodness. Hence the change has to be specified. I have tried out a plausible fiction or two here, to show that so far one can assign no clear content to the possibility of men's being built wholly good. But maybe some determinist will dream up a plausible fantasy to establish his point. But let him do so: for so far the Utopia Thesis is wrapped in cloud.

Again it might be argued, from the side of theism, that this discussion works against angels just as much as it works against the possibility of wholly good men. If we cannot make sense of noncosmomorphic worlds we cannot make sense of angelic worlds. Maybe so: though angels, qua messengers of God, could share in the intelligibility of God. But that takes us too far afield.

Conclusion—My anthropological fiction seems to bring out the point that moral discourse is embedded in the cosmic status quo (or even more narrowly, in the planetary status quo). For it is applied to a situation where men are beings of a certain sort. Thus the abstract possibility that men might have been created wholly good loses its clarity as soon as we begin to imagine alternative possible universes. If then the Utopia Thesis is quite unclear, it cannot assert anything intelligible about God. And so it cannot serve as part of an antitheistic argument. There remains of course many serious difficulties for the theist in regard to human evil. But the Utopia Thesis is not one of them.

Or not yet. We shall see how the science fiction goes.

SELECTED
BIBLIOGRAPHY

Aiken, H. D., "God and Evil: A Study of Some Relations Between Faith and Morals," *Ethics,* Vol. LXVIII, No. 2 (1958).

Aquinas, Thomas, *Summa Contra Gentiles,* Book III, Chap. 71.

————, *Summa Theologica,* Part I, Ques. 25, Art. 6 and Part I, Ques. 49.

St. Augustine, *City of God,* Book XI, Secs. XX-XXIII and Book XII, Secs. III-VII.

————, *Enchiridion,* Chaps. 3-8 and 26.

Bayle, Pierre, "Manicheism," *The Dictionary Historical and Critical of Mr. Peter Bayle,* revised, corrected, and enlarged by Mr. Des Maizeaux. London, 1737.

Book of Job

Bradley, F. H., *Appearance and Reality,* Chap. 17. Oxford: The Clarendon Press, 1893.

Buber, Martin, *Good and Evil.* New York: Charles Scribner's Sons, 1952.

Ducasse, C. J., *The Philosophical Scrutiny of Religion,* Chap. 16. New York: The Ronald Press Company, 1953.

Ferré, Nels, *Evil and the Christian Faith.* New York: Harper and Row, Publishers, 1947.

Flew, Antony, "Divine Omnipotence and Human Freedom" and "Theology and Falsification," *New Essays in Philosophical Theology,* A. Flew and A. MacIntyre, eds. New York: The Macmillan Company, 1955.

Laird, John, *Mind and Deity,* Chap. 6. London: George Allen & Unwin, 1941.

Leibniz, G. W., *Theodicy.* See especially the first of the "Essays on the Justice of God and the Freedom of Man in the Origin of Evil" and also the first Appendix.

Lewis, C. S., *The Problem of Pain.* New York: The Macmillan Company, 1944.

Maimonides, Moses, *A Guide to the Perplexed,* Part III.

McCloskey, H. J., "The Problem of Evil," *The Journal of Bible and Religion,* Vol. XXX, No. 3 (1962).

McTaggart, John, *Some Dogmas of Religion,* Chap. 6. London: Edward Arnold, Ltd., 1906.

Mill, John Stuart, "Nature," *Nature and Utility of Religion,* G. Nakhnikian, ed. New York: The Liberal Arts Press, 1958.

Mitchell, Basil, "Theology and Falsification," *New Essays in Philosophical Theology,* A. Flew and A. MacIntyre, eds. New York: The Macmillan Company, 1955.

Petit, François, *The Problem of Evil.* New York: Hawthorn Books, Inc., 1959.

Pike, Nelson, "God and Evil: A Reconsideration," *Ethics,* Vol. LXVIII, No. 2 (1958).

Pringle-Pattison, A. S., *The Idea of God,* Chap. 20. Oxford: The Clarendon Press, 1917.

Royce, Josiah, *Religious Aspects of Philosophy,* Chap. 22. New York: Harper and Row, Publishers, 1885.

———, *Studies in Good and Evil,* Chap. 1. New York: Appleton-Century-Crofts, Inc., 1889.

Spinoza, Benedict, *Ethics,* Appendix to Part I.

Tsanoff, Rodoslav, *Religious Crossroads,* Chap. 16. New York: E. P. Dutton & Co., Inc., 1942.

Voltaire, *Candide.* (Especially relevant to Leibniz' *Theodicy.*)

Wisdom, John, "God and Evil," *Mind,* Vol. XLIV. No. 173 (1935).